Susannah,

Connecting with you
is A Blessing !!!

Keith Blanchard

11/11

THE

DIVINE

PRINCIPLE

THE DIVINE PRINCIPLE

ANCHORING HEAVEN ON EARTH

———————————

Keith Blanchard

(Yah Nah Vah)

First published by AuthorHouse 10/15/04

Printed in the United States of America

ISBN: 978-1-615-39472-2

Editor/Copyshaper: Stella Steele
Additional editing: Brian Steel, Stacy McKinley
Cover design by: Keith Blanchard and Rikk Flohr
Contact: info@fleetingglimpse.com
Cover assistance: Fleeting Glimpse Images

To contact The Center of Light:
Send email to: info@thedivineprinciple.com
Web Site: www.thedivineprinciple.com
MySpace: myspace.com/divinelavender

This book is dedicated to my son Eden Sky's arrival on Earth
and to the loving memory of those dear ones who have left it —
Cheryl Blanchard Taylor, Amanda Larpenter,
Andrew Thompson, Jeff Opp, and Amber Shelton.

CONTENTS

PREFACE

It's August 19, 2003, as I sit at my computer to write about how this book came to be.

As I reflect back on my life from my present vantage point, I can see that a deliberate hand has affected it always, but because I was unaware of its influence, I lived in an ongoing state of turmoil and fear. At various times in my childhood I did actually manage to slow down enough to sense these promptings, especially when I served as an altar boy every Sunday in church. Then, when I was a teenager, I even attended seminary school and thought seriously of becoming a Catholic priest. But that isn't what I really wanted it seems, because I soon reverted to my unconscious ways.

As the years passed with their many ups and downs, I came to regard the few good things that happened to me as my life's highlights, and I despised the bad ones because I thought they only proved that things always got worse. And

I was perpetually worried about how, or if, this kid was ever going to find his way.

In my late twenties I finally had to admit that I was living with way too much chaos inside and all around me. Since nothing else I'd done had ever worked to help me get things in order, I decided to at least try to surrender the rest of my life to God's Will. After I'd made my decision to get more faith in my life, I went about living it, even though I didn't know for sure if anything was ever going to change for the better.

It was around then that God got my attention big time, but He didn't come to me as you might imagine. There was no burning bush. I didn't have a talk with George Burns. And Jesus didn't appear above my bed. No, God came to me through someone that I'd been involved with for ten years.

Towards the end of our relationship, things were not at all good between this woman I claimed to love and myself. In fact they were terrible! All we did was fight. Our relationship had become one of no communication, patience or tolerance. It was just awful because, through all our troubles, I still loved her. And through it all, I prayed to God that we could find some peace.

I should have been clear about what I asked for because, to my amazement, one day my longtime love told me that she wanted to end our relationship. That began a landmark period for me, even though, through my pain, I couldn't see it at the time. Now I know that that's when I truly recognized God as a presence in my life for the first time.

Early on in this time of transition, I began to meditate every day in an effort to find some sense of stillness. To help myself stay in that peaceful space and to make myself available for any God-manifestation that might come along, I soon intensified my practice. Whatever I was doing must have worked because one day God actually spoke to me — and *I could actually hear His Voice!*

"Good morning, Keith!" was what I heard when I was abruptly awakened on that cloudy June morning in 1996. In my dazed state, I thought that my wife at the time or a friend was nudging me to get up so they could tease me for being so lazy. But when I sat up in bed I could see no one there.

Then the Voice spoke again, "I am inside of you. Yes, it is true that I am here with you and you are here with Me!"

At that moment, I fell back on the bed, my eyes closed, and I found myself standing in the Presence and Light of the Divine. As I tried to collect myself, my first thought was, "What do I *do* with this?" The Voice responded, "I shall tell you. Sit on the sofa, press RECORD on your tape player, close your eyes and let your mouth move." I did what the Voice instructed and to my astonishment, out poured volumes of the most far-out material I'd ever heard. When I opened my eyes after that first God-session, all I could think was, "Oh s**t!"

Later that afternoon when I shared what had happened with my then brother-in-law Kevin, he suggested, "Keith, maybe you should go meet with Robin." Robin was an acquaintance of his with the gift of sight — a psychic. Kevin assured me that Robin was genuine and very good at what he did and that he could most likely tell me much more about the phenomena that had begun to appear in my life. Though

I'd never met this person before, I determined to let what he said help me decide what to do next.

I made an appointment to see Robin as soon as I could. When I got to his home the next afternoon, he answered the door, greeted me warmly and invited me upstairs to the sanctuary he'd created where our reading would take place. As we got settled, Robin asked me to tell him my zodiac sign and then asked to look at my left palm. To this day I remember the first thing he said, "You are being told to write a book, aren't you?" "What! Oh my God, then it's real!" I was so blown away that I had a hard time concentrating on the rest of the reading. In fact, I don't remember any of it except what he said about writing that book.

I left Robin's house still not certain about what I was going to do other than begin to write down all the words that the Voice was speaking into my mind. Over the next few years, questioning the whole time why I was doing this, something kept happening that helped me to accept my fate. "What was that?" you ask. "What helped you finally and wholly surrender to your path?"

Well, after hearing the Voice for a while, I began to have strong premonitions — visions — that would fade in and out as I diligently transcribed on the computer all that was coming to me. It was as if God was handing me a complete plan that told me what I needed to do in order to help myself and others.

Those visions have continued to reinforce my trust throughout this entire process. And the more I've let myself trust, the easier it's been for me to hear and feel the Love that could only be emanating from that wondrous Being.

Now I humbly and gratefully share with you, my readers, all the incredible things He told me — the splendor, joy and wisdom of all I've received. And I wish for you, too, a life full of the love, peace, prosperity and bliss I've come to accept.

In love and service,

Keith Blanchard

*Embrace each of your
brothers and sisters
without discrimination
and treat them with
the same Love
I bestow upon you.*

MAKE NO MISTAKE...

MAKE NO MISTAKE ABOUT WHO I AM

I
Am
God.

I have no particular name; they all belong to Me. I am all things—All that is. I am the Universal Generator of Supreme Knowledge and Divine Energy. I am You! I am everything you can perceive and everything you cannot. I am the Choreographer of the Human Dance. I am the Conductor of the Cosmic Symphony. I am the Universal Playwright. I am the Almighty, the Most High, the Creator. I am Love. I am all Teachers who have ever come bringing information about love and peace. I am Jesus the Christ. I am the Buddha. I am Krishna. I am Sathya Sai Baba. I am the All-knowing, All-pervasive and

1

All-seeing Eye. I am Clarity. I am Union. I am the Eternal. I am the Absolute in and of all things. I am the Atma, the Soul and the Tree of Life. I am the Only One. I am Jehovah. I am that I am.

God

Am

I.

I come to you imbued with Love and Light, Joy and Might! My purpose is of the highest calling: to give you the precious gifts of My Words and My Love so that you can share them with others and inspire them to join you in carrying out My mission.

———•·—————

MAKE NO MISTAKE ABOUT WHO YOU ARE,
MY BELOVED KEITH

Hello, My Friend, how are you today?
"Fine." (thinking to himself)
I am waiting...
"For what?" (still thinking to himself)
For you to begin.
"Begin what?"
Transcribing what *you* have to say, Keith. This book will be unbalanced if no one knows what you are thinking.
"You're right — I have so many questions!"
I know. That is why this is your forum as well, a place

for you to speak your own mind and heart. And I shall answer all that you ask, provided it serves you.

"Why me? Why did You come to me?"

Why not you? Keith, You have worked long and hard to get to where you are now—open to all possibilities of Spirit. You are ready.

"For what?"

To help Me write a book about universal truth. Can you deny that you have elected to come to the earth plane to carry out this very purpose—to share My words with as many people as you can?

"I'm a little overwhelmed, but, no, I can't deny that I've sought this path."

I know that My recent arrival in your life has seemed both a blessing and a curse—a rose under your nose and a thorn in your side. When I first made audible contact, you were very excited, but you were also quite frightened because you did not know just how to handle what was happening to you. You had moments when you thought you were special, and moments when you feared that you were schizophrenic.

"Yeah, I've definitely been through a lot!"

Yes, all your life I have watched you bounce back and forth between these two extremes in hopes of finding your True Self. I come to you now because you have exhibited such passion to live a better life. I come to you because of your newly awakened love for Me—and because of My Love for you.

You see, you and I are not different at all, for we both

share the same intention — to chip away at the beliefs that you thought were set in stone and to carve you into the most beautiful masterpiece ever known — God.

Keith, I cannot begin to tell you the ways your life will change, nor can I allay all your worries about what may happen when this book circulates. In fact, it is likely that you will be deluged with confusing feelings. But I can tell you that I am here to help with all that may be troubling you and that, for the rest of your life, I shall guide you so that you can play your part in making the world a better place.

Even though, right now, you have no idea what you will do with what you are beginning to receive, it is enough for you to know that the message comes from God. Fret not about those who may doubt you or scoff at what you say, for they may not be ready to hear it. You can put your mind and heart at ease nonetheless, knowing that everyone walks the path at their own pace.

As I pour My Light into your mind and My Love into your heart, just make a supreme effort to remain open, relaxed and aware in every moment, even when I am speaking directly to others. Only then can you integrate all My information.

"How am I doing so far? I mean, the path I'm on?"

You have already done some mighty fine work on yourself, Beloved, but now the *real* work begins!

Between now and forever, I ask that you gather people, one at a time if you have to, but gather them do. Embrace each of your brothers and sisters without discrimination and treat them with the same Love I bestow upon you, be they "enemies," friends, relatives or strangers. Embrace every little spark of God.

Your journey will be smoother if you accept the fact that, through everything, I am here.

"I'm so glad to be able to ask You all the questions I've wanted to ask if I ever got the chance. Y'know, the ones that could change the world if we had those answers."

Well, you are not the only one with questions. Here are some I ask *you* to ponder:

From whence did you come?

Did you have an identity before you were born?

Why were you born?

What is this energy that was given a name at birth?

Who are you now?

Where are you going?

———————◆———————

MAKE NO MISTAKE ABOUT WHO YOU ARE,
MY BELOVED ONES

It is no accident that you hold this book in your hands! Now that you have it, I encourage you to take full advantage of it, for within its pages you will find everything you need to understand your True Self and your relationship to the Spirit you call by many names. The words My scribe has written herein are to prepare you for the change that is already underway. Consider this work an instruction manual for your return to God.

Those of you who choose to live by the ideas and principles I present herein will awaken from your dream of separation and shift into a higher reality that will enable you to consciously re-unite with Me. So I implore you to not only read these words with your eyes, but with your heart, for doing so will open you even more to receiving My Intent and My Energy—All that I am.

I have miracles for all of you. Seek them with sincere intention and I shall grant you the awareness that will cause them to appear.

Fortunate are you to be the frontrunners and to read about the Divine changes soon to come. Blessed are you to receive the Divine Principles that will empower you. Privileged are you to learn about the return of Master Jesus and other Masters of My Most Holy Light.

*My stance of
unconditional Love
defines
Who I am.*

WALK INTO THE ONE

Are you ready to begin your journey, Keith?

"I am so ready! What are we gonna talk about first?" (excitedly)

Webster's Dictionary.

"Huh...why?"

Because it tells of your language, and its words will help Me to clearly and precisely convey my ideas. Using this resource will give you a deeper and broader perspective of any principle I am targeting.

"Okay."

Here is our first definition:

Union

An alliance for mutual benefit. The bringing together of two entities into a whole.

———————◆———————

Scripture speaks of God as the Living Word, the Essence of life itself." In the beginning was the Word. And the Word was with God, and the Word was God." (John 1:1) How hard can it be to see how people create grief, fear and division within themselves by denying this most profound truth?

I come to you now to teach you how to accept Me in order that you may replace your sorrow with joy and your trepidation with love; to help you supplant separation with unity. You see, when you live in the Love state, not only are you in My Presence—it is there that you *consciously* merge with Me. But we have to get you there first, Dear One.

It may be difficult for you to understand that

I

Am

Here

communicating with you telepathically. But, at the very least, you cannot deny that we are having this talk, can you?

"You're right about that!"

But you are not the only one I am with. I talk and walk with everyone on every continent every day. It is just that many do not know how to recognize Me because they believe I am in Heaven, not on Earth. Then there are those who are completely satisfied with knowing that I exist, but care nothing whatsoever about doing the work required to see Me.

"Sometimes I can't even see You myself. I mean, I sometimes still buy into the belief that I'm having a relationship with others, not with You."

Yes, you still have a tendency to separate others from God. But not letting yourself see Me in others only brings grief and fear into play for you. The fact is, I am with everyone personally and directly all the time.

"So no matter what the scenario, even in an argument with someone else, I'm fighting You?"

Yes, it is true you are resisting Me, but you are really just fighting yourself. This is why an argument can never be won, because the fight is yours and yours alone. Has going against the grain ever worked for you?

"It sure hasn't. That's why I'm concentrating on learning how to stay in the present moment."

So now that you are living this way, do you find that things are changing for you?

"Yes, they are, and it's about time."

No, Keith, it is not *about* time, it is *beyond* time. I say again that you are eternal, sustained by the Word (Om). My great joy will be when you see just how beautiful you are, how vibrant, and how precious your life is to Me. When that day comes, you will discover within you the world, the cosmos—God, the One Life Force that permeates everything. Quite fascinating, is it not?

"I want that so badly and, yes, I'm very intrigued!"

Well, here is your chance, Beloved, because you are being blessed with the opportunity to achieve your poten-

11

tial by getting to know Me through you, as you. I want you to know that I find it a great privilege to know you through Me, as Me.

"What do I say to something like that except that I'm honored to be a part of Your message!"

Just to let you know, I have been trying to get your attention for a long, long time. Now, as you let yourself open, you will soon begin to see who I *really* am.

"I'll do my best."

I know how immense this challenge is for you because, since you were born, you have been instilled with the idea of separation. Because of this feeling, you have often forgotten your kinship with Me and that has caused you more grief in the long run than any dilemma you may have been confronting. But I bring you a love offering full of information to help you remember the peace you sometimes tend to overlook.

"I'm the first to admit that I need it."

On our spiritual excursion, we shall cover the basic principles that are imperative for your growth. We will first form a solid foundation of understanding so that we can then move on firm footing to achieve the peace that you seek. Once you know yourself as a chip off My ol' block, you will then see how you have always had the power to create the best reality for yourself.

Thought energy is the primal force that gives birth to life in all its forms. Just because you are not aware of your thoughts after they leave your head, it does not mean that your thoughts die.

The moment you entertain any thought, the universe begins to work toward its manifestation. Everything is affected because all is One—the same Body, the same Being. For you to understand more fully that everything is of One Energy, we must start with the Soul and work our way outward.

Know that in every human being there are more bodies than just the physical one, and there is much more taking place than meets the eye.

THE SPIRIT SELF OR BODY: The Spirit is the aspect that descends into a body to partake of the human experience. It creates and governs all that is you. The Spirit works in conjunction with your own awareness to bring about what is beneficial for your evolution so that you may one day embody the Divine Principle.

THE MENTAL SELF OR BODY: This aspect provides you with the ability to reason. What I mean by reason is having the capability to consciously recognize what is right for you in any situation. It is the part of you that creates by thought and choice.

THE EMOTIONAL SELF OR BODY: This aspect is denser than the spiritual and mental bodies and is responsible for physical expression. It influences all the actions and reactions triggered by your pleasure/pain memories. Its enormous power brings what you are choosing into the certainty of being.

THE PHYSICAL SELF OR BODY: This is what most people think they are—the body. But really, your physical body is just the vehicle for the other bodies. It lets you move freely in the world while you work to align your personality with your Soul. It is your individuality. Your physical self allows you to come together with others to share life experiences.

All these aspects make up the human entity. Even though they are different, they have one thing in common: they are all made up of energy. It is through such synergy that the physical, emotional and mental bodies connect to the all-pervading Spirit.

On the earth plane, almost everyone perceives himself or herself as an individualized unit, separate from others. Such spiritual deficiency promotes spiritual dyslexia—a view of reality as outer to inner, rather than inner to outer. This perception is in error because, at the subatomic level, there is no separation whatsoever. Everything is just energy fluxing at Godspeed, briefly bumping around, then taking off to somewhere else.

Believe it or not, the human body is 99.9999% empty space. The other .00001% (matter) is empty space as well. Matter consists of random blips of energy and informational discharges that solidify into a three-dimensional hologram, thus creating the illusion of solidity.

I know that grasping this concept has been challenging for you in the past, Dear One. But are you finally beginning to see how everyone is of One Body that branches into many seemingly separate bodies upon the physical plane?

"Yes, I think I am."

The more you can see this truth, the more your tendency to judge anything will diminish because you will understand that *everything is you*. When you cast judgment, not only do you bring about division from others— you deepen the conscious breach between yourself and the One Cosmic Body. When you judge, love begins to decay and fear begins to expand.

Now, even though I describe separation as a truth in and of itself, in truth, it is not real. Nothing can ever leave My sight—that is the real truth. I live in such wholeness that I even hold together the things you may see as separate.

Here is an exercise for you. Look at your hand. Do you see it as a hand with separate fingers?

"Yes."

Because of those empty spaces you see between them, you think that one finger has no connection to the others. This is but a perception of separation caused by your lack of focus on the entire hand, which, after all, is where your fingers extend from in the first place. Your hand represents the place where all things connect and originate—God. This simple lesson should lift your awareness beyond any deception. Do you understand it?

"I've really gotta hand it to You. You've explained it so well that even I get it!" (slyly smiling)

Now let us look at the connection you have with the Earth and all the life upon it.

Again, I ask you to reflect on your body and see it as one living organism housing billions of cells—skin cells, liver cells, brain cells, blood cells and so on—all of them encapsulated in one wrapping of flesh.

This holds true for Earth as well, where there are billions of individual cells called people who differ from one another in personality, appearance, sex and race. Humans are embraced by a much larger organism — Earth. Humans are to Earth as cells are to humans. From micro to macro, the universal design is the same.

Atomic→Cellular→Body→World→
Solar→Galactic→Stellar→Universal

All systems spin around one central source. Atoms and cells have elements spinning around one central source called the nucleus; and you and Earth spin around one central source called the Sun. The solar system revolves around the Milky Way galaxy with that huge star cluster at its center. Galaxies rotate around the cosmos, and the universe revolves around God — the Great Central Sun. I know you have heard the expression: "He thinks the world revolves around him." Well, this *is* the truth of it. Everything revolves around Me, for it is I who spins all into life.

"It sounds pretty simple, I mean, as far as how You've laid things out."

Yes, it is so simple that, without forcing anything, Truth brings about the natural flow of life and light that allows the Divine to be omnipresent. This is just the way it is! I do not judge it, for it is what it is.

"Do You think I'll ever get there in this lifetime?"

That is entirely up to you, Keith. Know that, even now,

WALK INTO THE ONE

you have what it takes to grasp the complexity of the universe and to anchor the Divine Principle if you accept living in love as your abiding criterion.

With this new awareness of your relationship to Earth, other human beings and God, you now have the ability to understand all that is taking place in the era that you are living in. I share with you this truth of your connectedness to bring you stability and to provide you with a deeper comprehension of the way things will play out in these transitional times.

"You mean things will get worse before they get better?"

I did not say that, you did. But I can tell you that your unity with God and Earth will only aid you when the wheels of Spirit really begin to roll.

"That sounds both promising and ominous. What dynamic is taking place now?"

Earth's energy is beginning to shift dramatically and it is lifting at an exponential rate. The pace of life is accelerating like never before and in this age of computer technology, when new phenomena quickly become obsolete, most people find it tough just to keep up. But it is very important for all of you to update yourselves and absorb as much information as possible. After all, who do you think is behind this idea that you call the Information Age?

"That goes without saying."

Does it now?

"Well, it's obvious to me — You are!"

So why is the world so reluctant to use it to its fullest capacity?

"Ouch!"

Let Me put it this way: When humanity finally does get around to taking in what I have been saying for eons, world peace will be yours.

"So what should we call this time we're living in — the End, the Beginning, the New Age, the Golden Age, Revelation, Armageddon, the Rapture — what?"

It matters not to Me what you call it. What does matter is for you to believe with all you have that I am blanketing you and Earth with Love's vision so that humanity can see what has been created, how it is working and what needs to be re-cycled for your further expansion.

You must know that the "closer" I get to you, the more the Law of Cause and Effect will be in play. Said another way, as My Light pierces the illusion of time and space, everything about you will be unmasked to reveal your shadow self, your own illusion.

"Are You saying that cause and effect will not be separate and that our thoughts will suddenly begin to manifest?"

Right, kiddo! As the world keeps moving down its time-line, reality will indeed begin to immediately manifest from thought, because God-power is wending Its way through every Soul on the planet—making now the perfect time to manifest your own life's desires. But before we can truly work and play together, I must first mirror to each of you with all My Love exactly who you are as a think-ing, feel-ing, do-ing, be-ing being.

"So that's how the universe functions?"

Yes, absolutely. The whole system of Creation works in harmony, constantly learning and updating, ever expanding. And I am ready to reveal to all of you the progress we have made.

"So, if we're all partly responsible for creating this magnificent universe, why did any of us choose to consciously leave its grandeur and come to live on Earth?"

Just for the "hell" of it. Let Me ask you, are you having any fun?

"At this point in my life, I'd say I am — pretty much."

Well then, that is enough. We shall continue our discourse tomorrow.

———◆———

How are you today, Keith?

"I'm just fine, thanks."

I am ready to transmit more information. Are you ready to transcribe it?

"I'm ready, but something's been bugging me all night."

I know. You have been wrestling with why I said "hell" yesterday.

"I didn't want people asking me a question that I didn't have the answer to."

Well, I can give you several of them.

First, I experience no guilt when I combine letters in a way that some call bad. You are the ones that react and your doing so last night just proves My point.

Second, I am only interested in results, and if using 'hell' produces a desired one, then so be it. Anyway, Who do you think created all those dirty words you throw around?

Third, let Me answer your question with another question. You see what is going on; how do you think most people find life on Earth?

"I see Your point."

Let Me remind you that My existence is truly Divine. This implies that life for anyone not consciously connected to Me...

"...can sometimes be hell. I get it."

The problem you are having is that you have gotten so wrapped up in the drama of life being just too much that you have forgotten to look to Me for relief. What I am trying to do here is unleash My Reality within you so that you can have your relief *and* your fun.

I am granting you awareness so that you can finish what we started and experience My Glory at a conscious level. All you need to do to be a conscious part of our great creation (and begin to have My kind of fun) is look within your own heart. In this readily available place is where you will find Me.

As I just illustrated above, all things in the universe are individual cells of God. As I embody you, you embody God. This is the sole/Soul reason you are here: to activate and anchor the Divine upon the Earth's physical plane.

"*You* may be having a blast on the cosmic level, but from where I sit, things are not always so peachy."

Yes, you are right, Keith. From My point of view, I am on a fun-filled journey. I shall effort to make My utterances more down to Earth so that you can better understand and ultimately get to Heaven yourself.

"I'd appreciate that."

No problem.

There is enormous potential for unpleasant things to manifest in your life, but they need not necessarily come into being. You said it correctly: as Love energy continues to lift, all things will quicken into manifestation. So if you wish to avert any adversity, you must clear yourself of any hate, guilt and fear you are holding on to. If these obstacles are not addressed, trouble will continue to show up for you on a regular basis.

It has been said that when the bad moon rises on people, God is testing them. This is completely nonsensical because such an assumption makes Me out to be the tempting devil that I most definitely am not.

It is ludicrous for people to think that I would tempt or tease them or play any part in their bad choices and the consequences that follow. When it comes down to the owning of a situation they may find themselves in, they want no part of it, so they play the "The devil made me do it!" card in a futile attempt to transfer their own response-ability onto a figment that does not exist.

These Divine/diabolical tests are given Soul→soul to generate experiences and to provide some Self↔self-reflection. I have no hand in such trivial matters. The fact that lessons come back around again and again only points out that people have not yet resolved specific negative energies.

But if you choose, Keith, you can own, integrate and

21

transcend your own "stuff" and re-unite with your Soul. Indeed, this re-union *must* take place before you can ever know God. But you see, Beloved, what you decide to do really does not matter to Me because, in the end (which, like the devil, does not exist), all creation will consciously return to Me. So why not go ahead and live your life with style, fun and integrity—for these are some of Love's vital components.

"May I ask a couple of questions?"

That is one. (chuckling) Yes, of course, ask.

"What constitutes Love and can anything exceed the parameters of Love?"

The answers are very simple. First, if you do not use your freewill to impinge upon someone else's, you are exercising My Love. Second, My Love knows no parameters. It transcends all boundaries of time, space and judgment. It adheres to no rules pertaining to this or that. I do not judge something to be anything other than Myself.

"But what I was taught..."

Never mind what you were taught! I know this may not sound like the god you have been used to; nonetheless, these are the constructs of My Love.

"When trials show up in my life, does it mean that I've been abusing my freewill? Is that why I sometimes feel You are testing me?"

I have never tested anyone. The truth is, you are testing yourself. Your unhappy experiences have come about because you have not yet worked through your karma. But if you wish Me to, I will test you here and now.

"No — not that!"

Relax, this will not hurt. (laughing)

"What do You have in mind?"

A test, like you had in school.

"But I did lousy in school. I failed a lot of classes. In fact, I didn't even graduate!"

Well, Beloved, My test is designed for you to pass! Do you not wish to put to rest the questions you are having about God, you and us, so you can get to a better understanding of the Law of One?

Just one note: for each question only one answer is possible — the correct one, the highest one. Prepare to earn an A+! The reward for your high grade is union. Know that you are so loved that failure is not an option. I await the moment when I place upon you that big gold star for scoring 100%.

Take a deep breath and relax. Ready?

"Yes."

Then we shall begin.

Who am I?

"God."

Can God read your mind?

"Yes."

Would I not have to be somehow connected to you to do this?

"Yes, of course."

Is the mind of God clear?

"Yes."

Is there anything that I have created without clarity? If so, what do you think it would be?

"No, I don't think anything could've come about if You were not clear."

Is God a perfect Being?

"Yes."

Is God capable of creating anything that is not perfect?

"No."

Who created you?

"You."

Who created Earth?

"You."

Who created the solar system, which is one of infinity?

"You."

And Who created the Milky Way galaxy, which is one of infinity?

"You."

Who created the universe?

"You did."

Who created God?

"No one."

And therefore . . . ?

"You just are?"

Yes. Always have been and always will be.

Who sustains your life?

"You."

Who sustains the life and movement of the solar system?

"You."

WALK INTO THE ONE

And Who sustains the life and movement of the Milky Way galaxy?

"You."

Who sustains the life and movement of the universe?

"You do."

Again, who sustains the life and movement of God?

"I can see now that everything — except You — is derived from You. So, I'm perplexed — what *are* You really?"

It would be more correct to ask what I am not, for there is no form that is not Me and there is no name that I do not bear. God is not My name, though the word does invoke an image of the Highest Authority. What I am is the Ultimate Awareness. What I am is Perpetual, Infinite Potential.

Surely you can understand that everything born of Infinite Potential has within it its own spark of Infinite Potential. Everything has infinite potential to become Infinite Potential. But to become invincible like Me, you must go deep within and reach for that Infinite Potential yourself.

"I think I may actually understand this!" (amazed at himself)

So you are not perplexed after all?

"No, I guess I'm not."

You see, by your intent to go within and seek, you have pierced your confusion at last. You have just become introduced to your own Infinite Potential. Now let us see what you do next.

As clearly as there are rewards for going within yourself

for sustenance, there are definite consequences for going outside. When you reach out to grab the world, you are vulnerable to its influences and the rules that apply on the physical plane. It is there that you encounter the many distractions and temptations that result in your conscious disconnection.

Looking to the temporal world for what you think you need implies a belief that you are lacking something. I ask you, why must you reach outward for fulfillment? You can never reach your Infinite Potential and power that way.

"Hmmm..." (thinking about how often he reaches outward)

Do you understand that *God is Life Itself* and is not separate from Creation?

"Yes, because if that were a possibility, all would cease to exist."

Seems to Me that you are getting the hang of it. The reason you and many sometimes find life so challenging is because you give credence to the idea that the world outside is something other than you. It is that which has caused so many of you to feel so alone. But—here is the kicker—all of you have the potential to tap into the Self that connects you to Me.

"Are You telling me that I'm just like You in every way?"

Let us say that you are already embodying many of My Principles.

"Like what?"

Like your innate ability to create a life of quality instead of one of mediocrity. As Scripture says: "You are created in

WALK INTO THE ONE

the image and likeness of God." (Genesis 5:1)

"I used to think that that meant You thought me into being and made me to look kind of like You."

If you only knew how many people think that. (laughing)

"That *is* pretty darned funny." (chuckling)

But there is more truth inherent in this than first meets the eye. You yourself put it nicely just a moment ago: it means that you cannot separate from the things you have brought forth in your life, lest they cease to be.

To further My point, let us continue that test I was giving you to see what happens when you separate yourself from your creations.

What happens if you remove your life force (yourself) from your checking account?

"It's no longer my checking account. It closes."

What happens to a relationship when you break it off?

"It's no longer a relationship."

What happens if you separate yourself from anything?

"I guess it would no longer be a part of my reality."

Do you find that your life has peace, joy, trust, love, compassion, acceptance, understanding, patience, and sharing?

"In many aspects of my life, I'm very happy. In others, there is definitely room for improvement."

Are you moving intentfully in that direction?

"I do my best to follow through, but I still procrastinate doing some things."

Why do you think you procrastinate?

"You're trying to tell me something here, aren't You?"

Yes, I am waiting to see if you dare do something about that habit of yours?

"This sounds like one of the traps I thought You were setting for me a couple of times before. But this time I don't want to be snared! By the way, didn't You say that You don't tempt?"

That is right, I do not. But, right now, you are the exception to that rule. (picking on him)

"You sound just like my dad!"

Yes. He picks on people he loves. Your father, he is a great and generous man. Oh, and let us not forget your mom who is the epitome of a Divine mother. She has to be to put up with the two of you! (still teasing)

"So that's how it's gonna be, huh?"

What do you say we call a truce and get back to where we left off?

"If I only had more time, I'm sure I could come up with a good one."

Well, I have all the time there is, so go ahead, give it your best shot! (waiting)

"Oh, forget it!"

What is the matter, Keith?

"I couldn't think of anything. You probably stopped all my incoming thoughts."

Yes, I do have the ability to do that. But I will send you some images if it will make you feel better.

"That was quick. I just got one."

Okay, let Me have it.

"What in Heaven's name were You thinking when You created the duckbilled platypus? I thought You were always clear!" (laughing hard)

Where did that come from? It was not Me that sent you that image!

"I have my ways of finding out what I need to know."

Got Me! So, do you feel better?

"Much! I'm ready to get back to work. Where did we leave off?"

Why do you think you procrastinate?

"You're still trying to tell me something here, aren't You?"

Yes, but this time I am waiting for you to tell Me how I can help you.

"Oh, I've got it! You're waiting for me to ask You for some help in letting go."

Ah, Beloved, just as I suspected, you *are* a good student! Now, just a couple more questions.

If I am complete Love, is there anything I have created that is not an extension of My Self?

"Absolutely nothing!"

And, finally, if God is Love and you are God, why is fear a part of *your* experience and not a part of *Mine?*

"I have no earthly idea!" (trying to be funny)

I have to admit that is a good one, but not as good as the platypus!

Keith, fear is nothing more than that—a fear. Time and again, the mistakes that you have made by living without Divine Principles have perpetuated your fear cycle and have left you with all those feelings of lack. Remember, whenever you buy into one of your fears it is because you have a false sense of emptiness. I will break this down for you.

You can say that fear is...

False
Emptiness
Actualizing
Reality

...a space void of Love—God—You. Fear is a self-created block that constricts you and keeps you from becoming open to the Divine Self that wants to pour through you and bring you fulfillment. So you see, even though you do have God qualities, fear is the one thing I do not share with you, for it has no connection at all to anything that is Love. The physics here should not be too complex to understand —fear is yours and yours alone.

Later on, when I share My Divine Principles and you begin to put them to use, you will see your fears dwindle. Living these Divine Principles will keep you focused on God as your only reality. Applying them at every opportunity will help you to become a part of the all-pervading reality of Love—the Living Truth.

"Sometimes it seems that, at the very time I'm feeling fearful, my fear is protecting me from something."

Does it seem as if it is protecting you from the very thing that you are afraid of?

"Yeah, that's exactly what it's like!"

What you have not yet realized is that your fear does not protect you. What it does is complicate the very scenarios you are efforting to simplify. You think that being afraid keeps you out of harm's way in a crisis, but what it does is throw you directly into its path where you must repeat the lesson, no matter how long it takes.

"So tell me, is reincarnation real and, if it is, is fear the reason I've had to do it so many times?"

Yes. According to universal law, all actions spawned from a fearful place must come back around for review and resolution. If you do not clear your present self of past problems, you will be re-born again and again until you do resolve them.

The thing I must tell you is that reincarnation both does and does not exist. When Scripture speaks of "the Beginning and the End," it is to accommodate your current frame of reference. Its concepts have to be conveyed in this way because, at this point, you are only mindful of a linear timeline and cannot easily conceive of eternity.

"Yeah, that's a tough one to fathom alright!"

Well, try it now. Take few moments, Dear One, and meditate on eternity. When you are through, open your eyes.

"Okay, I'm done."

Tell Me, Dear One, how many Souls do you think there are? Take your time before you answer. Think about what you just experienced during your meditation.

"Um . . . there's only one, but It has many facets."

Yes, and in eternity those many facets or faces of the

One Universal Soul live all at once. So really, all there is *is* You (God). But your consciousness must flip-flop around and through the time-space continuum until you remember that.

Keith, you have lived many lifetimes only to find yourself here, now. Although you have lived in many different forms, none of them is what you are; for what you are is the Spirit that has lived, lives and will live forever.

"What have I done that has landed me in so many lives?"

In most of your incarnations you have chosen the world of the external and material over that of the spiritual, thus guaranteeing the repetition of your births and deaths.

But if you want to live eternally — where there are no more births and deaths, just life everlasting — you have to replace your fear with Love. Once you get to that level, your consciousness will no longer be interrupted, the cycle will no longer perpetuate. But, as of now, you are only the potential of what you can become.

"Whew, that's a lot to get!"

Yes, it is, My Friend, but I find I must often play with words to help you understand what I am conveying and, most especially, to enable you to grasp some inkling of the Wholeness that I am.

Look at the word

E-X-T-E-R-N-A-L

Notice its similarity to the word

E-T-E-R-N-A-L

Observe that there is just one difference: the "**X**" in the word eXternal crosses out and interrupts the flow of the word eternal.

This is exactly what happens to your consciousness when you choose to live in external mode. You cross out all your chances for eternity. And so the current of your life will go, until the time when you are able to live in unbroken flow. If you honestly seek union with Me, you must hold steadfastly to your intentions and be ever-vigilant. When you achieve this life-mode, then your next death cycle will be a Divine birth.

"Is that what it means to be re-born?"

Not quite, Beloved. Let Me be perfectly clear. Birth's intention is to not be born again and death's intention is to never again die. The intentions of both are the same — to give you every possible chance to consciously unify with All that is. Now, whether or not you choose to go along with this program is entirely up to you.

———◆———

It is vital that you begin to inform yourself on all matters, especially spiritual teachings from around the world. When you do, you will find all the doctrines you study are but jigsaw puzzle pieces waiting to be assembled. And when the puzzle finally does piece together, do not be surprised to see the image of My Face shining through.

You must not accept blindly that everything you have been taught or will hear is true. Figure things out for yourself by weighing the possibilities and probabilities of what is the likely Truth.

"Is there anything You don't know?"

Ah, I thought you would never ask. Yes, there is one thing God is ignorant of—fear. Because there is no reality in such energy, I do not dwell there. Still, I see what fear does to all of you. It eats away at you like cancer. If you do not expose yourselves to My Love's radiation, fear will only continue to overtake your bodies. When it becomes too much, you will be forced to create your deaths to escape your unbearable lives.

Dear Ones, when will it dawn on you that *wherever you go, you are still you!* Nothing changes if you do not change yourselves from within, with or without a body. So I say to each of you, if you are sincerely seeking a better life, take responsibility and take action by pulling your perception out from under your fear. Only then will you be able to live in peace and share your love with all things in My Creation.

Now back to the basics of Self-love. It begins with finding the part of you that is original—your innermost Being —and consciously reuniting with It. Discovering such a sense of Self will introduce into your own life the same power to manifest that Jesus and other Ascended Masters throughout time have demonstrated in theirs. And it will bring you into balance so that the same Divine energies with which they created miracles will be available for your use.

Once you cross your spiritual threshold you will be able to further honor the contract that you made with Spirit before you were born, because you will then know through experience that the Life Force within you is God. You will have no choice but to live your life as a love offering. After all, this is your purpose, Dear One—to anchor the Divine Principle in your day-to-day reality.

"I'd love to be able to do that!"

What on Earth do you think you have been doing all this time?

"What do You mean?"

Are you not the one writing a book called *The Divine Principle: Anchoring Heaven On Earth?* And have you not been working on this daily?

"How did I not connect the two?"

Because you had not fully realized that you were having a talk with God! Now that you have chosen to open to the truth of who you are, you can become My channel. I could not have entered your consciousness any other way.

"Why wasn't I taught all this stuff when I was younger?" (crossly)

Well, did it ever occur to you that I might have been saving you? Believe Me when I tell you that your timing is perfect. Yes, Beloved, your Christ Self orchestrated this pre-ordained path so that you would be ready to write My words at a time when they are needed most—now.

Besides, you have had some growing up to do. You have had to work through karma to learn, update and expand. And to your credit, you have taken these opportunities to begin to fall into alignment. All you have learned has not been in vain, My Friend.

"Thank You, I'm glad to hear that. But what about others? Why is alignment so difficult for them?"

Because most are still waging an ongoing war in their minds—that noisy battle between "right and wrong"—which has kept them rigidly locked in their "victim" position. Though you are now able to tune out much of your own mental static, know that most people have much more twisting of the dial to do before I can come in loud and clear for them too.

If one lives his/her whole life with a right/wrong point of view and uses past memories to handle present circumstances, the stillness and clarity necessary to make sound choices will never be available. I am not saying that that position is either right or wrong; I am saying it can only result in one of those two possible outcomes.

Ego keeps people strapped into the front car of their own emotional roller coaster on a ride that never ends, because just over every incline is another right/wrong scenario that launches them through those disorienting swoops and loops yet again. As long as people refuse to get off their judgment ride, they can never hope to plant their feet on the solid ground of peace.

Concepts of right and wrong are taught by and learned from parents, society and those who claim to be authorities on the subject of God's Word. But what if the true meaning of life is neither way? How on Earth can someone come to understand another alternative?

"Through a teacher who embodies it?"

Yes, I have sent many to the world to show you that

there is a way that is neither right nor wrong. In a beautiful world, unconditional love would do the influencing, for it is the most effective way I know of to create the peace that you seek. Those who have not heeded these teachers' examples are living in a right/wrong world, which is why they have such trouble agreeing about what is supposedly right or wrong.

One way for you to get what I am saying is by observing life partners who claim to love unconditionally, but who remain stuck in their conditional condition, arguing all the time.

Another prime example is the strife that exists among many of the world's nations, each standing firm on "our idea is right" and "your idea is wrong." This attitude inevitably leads to arguments, wars and continued separation—frustrating standoffs between those who would rather defend their own position than concede and compromise.

Keith, you have tended to engage in this dynamic frequently, have you not? Am I "right" in saying that you have not achieved the effect that you were hoping for?

"Yeah, You're 'right' about both. But what about the people who say that their right or wrong opinion is based on God's Law?"

What about them? You are going to come across people, especially some religious leaders, who support that opinion by saying "God has determined what is right and wrong and God is something to fear!"

It never ceases to amaze Me when I hear fear and God

in the same breath. The Scripture that says "Judge not, lest ye be judged" does not mean that I judge your wrongs, then punish you for your "sins." It means that when you judge, you judge yourself for the poor decisions you have made in the past, and you judge others for the faults you see in yourself.

I am not like you in this regard. I have no past to cast judgment upon, for it takes all My time just to be the Love necessary to sustain Creation. *My stance of unconditional Love defines Who I am!*

What defines the world is its present dilemma — figuring out how to catch the ultimate wave of universal law. Up until now, most of you have wiped out in all your attempts because you have not yet learned the laws that will let you hang ten and master that ride all the way to Spirit. But now that I see your desire to change, I will present them to you. I will place you atop My surfboard so that you can finally coast in and land on My peaceful shore.

THE LAW OF GRAVITY: How is that for a law?

"That's a good one."

Until you are a master, if you go against this law, serious trouble is certain to come your way. Jumped off any buildings lately?

"No, and I don't intend to."

THE LAW OF KARMA: You reap what you sow. Cause and effect. This law ensures a Divine Order, and keeps it that way. Your difficulty has been that, until recently, you did not know that you are the one responsible for creating your reality.

THE LAW OF ALL POSSIBILITIES: One of My favorites. The universe is a place where miracles are normal occurrences and all things have a right to be. What will make everything possible for you is the clarity you find by pursuing God. But if you choose to keep on bearing the burden of doubt, the hopelessness that accompanies it will assure that nothing promising will ever come your way.

THE LAW OF GIVING: To give is to receive: the Way of Christ. Your illusion of lack has caused you to be selfish and to take, take, take, thus ensuring your ongoing impoverishment.

THE LAW OF PURPOSE OR DHARMA: Find what your own role is in My grand scheme and perform it by allowing your Spirit's expression to live and work in your life. Going against this law will put you on a sure path to misery.

THE LAW OF DETACHMENT: To find fulfillment in the indwelling God, all idol worship must be abandoned. Being attached to the external world does not work because when its temporal things are no longer a part of your life, your happiness most assuredly leaves with them.

Very simply, these are My Laws. If you work with them, they will work for you. Ignore them and the simple becomes difficult. In a later chapter, I will offer even more guidelines for you to follow as you endeavor to live in Spirit.

"What about rules? Are there any?"

No. Just keep reflecting on what I said about The Law of Karma and that will keep you in order and eventually free you.

"Tell me again what's been binding me?"

Your mind. It is your prison and your ego is its warden! You stay locked up inside because you still listen to that keeper of fear and disregard My Laws. But from this day forth, you can pardon yourself from this life sentence by listening to Me and by accepting the fact that

I

Am

Here

and I am offering you the key to unlock your Spirit. All you must do is accept it and know that you truly deserve all that is good.

You must believe that the Christ *is* you and you must begin to live that belief so that you can marshal the power to move through the illusions of separation, disease and, ultimately, death that will continue to present themselves. Only your perception, there by choice, is what keeps you from doing that.

"Is there an original sin and, if so, what is it?"

That would be conscious separation from God. But conscious or not, *you cannot separate from Me.* And, despite your God-amnesia, your Higher Self remains ready to emerge so that you can become Love on Earth.

Another thing that keeps you from knowing the Self is the large dose of doubt you still carry from other lifetimes. When will you realize that doubt is a most destructive force to inflict upon yourself? What do you think prevents you from knowing?

"Confusion?"

Yes, but why are you confused?

"It's like there's a battle going on within me. I feel I know what's real, but my analytical mind still tries very hard to convince me otherwise. I guess I've allowed the stuff I've taken in since birth to rule all my decisions."

Yes, that internal struggle is what I meant earlier when I spoke about right and wrong. Confusion has shaped your every doubt; doubt has created your confusion and lack of clarity; fear has taken away your power to create the life you truly want. These are your only opponents. There are no others. The only way to win this game we are talking about is to stop playing it.

"How?"

Stop thinking that you yourself are incapable of creating something beautiful! When you doubt, you either move forward in time or back, away from the power of the here and now. Doubt always creates gravity, drag and dread, and, as soon as you entertain it, it stifles anything creative you are trying to will forth. Only when you trust that everything will fall into place, will you find real power.

"It's not that I don't trust. It's more that I don't know how to let go of doubt."

I know what you are trying to say, Dear One, so let Me suggest this:

Give yourself the gift of accepting—if only for a few minutes at a time at first—that you are in a state of knowing at all times, a state in which you can easily recognize whether or not there is doubt, whether or not there is trust, whether fear or Love is in charge of your life. Then begin to peg the power that doubt holds over you and use this to your advantage. If you notice doubt, just redirect your knowing to cancel it; realize that nothing can possibly manifest through it. Let the knowing part of you that so wants to blossom transform doubt into trust, then watch what happens. The knower within you, with the know-how to get you what you want, will silently emerge.

If you take your trust to the ultimate level, (by wanting nothing and trusting your Higher Self — God — with your entire life), Spirit will begin to move within you and give you something far beyond what you can dream up on your own.

You have heard the saying, "It takes one to know one." In such a way, the Self will see Its own Beautiful Self — the True Miracle — for I am everywhere.

As you endeavor to see and be My Miracle, you will come across many keys that fit many doors. But only one will release you from the emptiness you feel.

"Which one is it?" (knowing something's up)

The one that opens the door leading to the void where miracles can happen.

"But it's so scary to go there!"

I know you feel intimidated, but I assure you that if you are willing to go through hell to get to Heaven, the Divine that occupies these seemingly empty spaces will be revealed to you.

"That's easy for You to say."

Know that I do understand your reluctance to confront the abyss of your own demons. That being said, do it anyway, for

I

Am

Here

with you, in places where you are not yet present with yourself, to give you what only I can—the feeling that everything is okay. All you need to do is let go and expand your awareness until you recognize the sureness of that.

"Will You walk with me?"

Right by your side, Beloved.

Now close your eyes and think of something that is really troubling you. Just breathe in and out evenly for a few minutes to fall deeper into yourself. Take notice of any of those negative feelings that come up. Then, with your last exhale, release your troublesome thought to the universe and listen carefully. Do you hear it?

"Hear what?"

The soft voice of the Soul whispering Its wisdom into your heart?

"I've been able to do this before when I've meditated on some other issues, but I can't seem to consciously make the connection on this one."

Then you must go even deeper to discover where your demon dwells! When you find it, it will probably look like a scared child cowering in a corner. But do not be fooled by its appearance and do not attempt to offer it pity, because it can and will take advantage of you. If you must, use another intense visualization to yank your demon out of your subconscious, then offer it up to the Light of Consciousness and watch it melt like the vampires you have seen in the movies.

When you begin to see through all your illusions, the beauty that has always been there will humble you. The circle of life will then curve back within you and suddenly God will be present for you at a conscious level.

"What about my future lessons?"

When something happens that you know could potentially be with you for a long time, I suggest that you heed and heal it at the very moment it transpires.

"Please share with me how."

While an issue is new, it is still potential energy — it has not yet become static. But if you let it fester, it will put down deep roots in an effort to mire you in its illusion. The longer you/it stay/s frozen, the tougher the thaw will be.

I know that I have been telling you that everything is God, so you must be wondering how it is that "terrible" things can be God. What you perceive as terrible is not the reality of God, but an illusion created by you. What I am saying is that the mind can never open up enough to take God in, so you must open your heart in order to move out of any illusion and into My Reality.

"But how will I know when I'm there?"

You will know you are heart-centered when you begin to see a world made up of hues that you could never see before. Everything will appear different to you — as if illuminated. You will know you have become heart-centered when you notice that joy is residing within you full-time.

"That illumination thing's already happening a lot — where things seem to have that glow You've mentioned and everything looks like it's softly blending together. What I want to know is how to stay in that space longer."

I shall tell you how: Be conscious of keeping your breathing just as even and steady as you possibly can, not only when you are meditating, but all the time. When you begin to live your life with this relaxed, letting go kind of feeling and a willingness to lose everything to gain your Self, you will have joy and complete trust where there was none before, and that space you were looking to expand will do just that.

You must also stop reaching for other things first and then for God when it is convenient for you. Perhaps you have been trying to seek Me with all that wanting, but it is your idolatry that has actually kept you from My Bounty.

Another thing that keeps you and all separate from Me and My Goodness is the very thought that you *are* separate, along with pondering the fearful thought that you are not. Need I remind you that you came here with no-thing and you will leave with no-thing? In the meantime, cultivate, nurture and develop your Soul — because *that* you can take with you wherever you go. And whenever your intent needs adjusting, pull out your Bible and refer to this passage for guidance: "But seek ye first the Kingdom of God, and His Righteousness; and all things shall be added unto you." (Matthew 6:33)

———•◆•———

Christ, Buddha and many other Teachers have taught the message of unity with Spirit. And teachers still come, bearing the same message: *Look within to know God*. All of them say that the Profound cannot be found in a church nor in belief, but only in the temple of your heart.

"Would it be correct to say that the heart is a stargate?"

Yes, and when you traverse it, you will enter the Kingdom of Heaven where universal Love reigns. Once there, you will be overwhelmed by utter serenity. Meanwhile, daily meditation and prayer will help you to free yourself from the drag of time. Soon you will begin to feel much lighter because many obstacles that have made you stumble along your path will be cleared away.

"For sure I'll continue to meditate because I know my addictive personality and I know that if I hadn't found this path, I would've never been able to survive. I was playing way too many games and sometimes I still do."

I like games.

"Well, yes, but ..."

Loved One, if you wish to play a game—play the game that will spin you off the fear/time wheel once and for all! I cannot emphasize enough that you must always try to make your spiritual work fun, because having fun is what keeps you in that God state, totally unaware of time. Tell Me, when you are having fun, where does the time fly?

"Hey, it does seem to fly. Why's that?"

The bliss you feel causes time to disappear.

"Wow, that's really neat!"

Have you noticed how a heaviness often comes over you when you look at a watch or clock and realize there is something you feel you *have* to do that will take you away from your fun?

"Again, I ask why?"

Because your conscious link to God gets broken when you do something you would not choose to do, but do anyway. That is when you move from eternal fun to dreaded time. When this happens, it only means that you have shifted from your heart to your head—from Love to fear.

I ask you, Keith, why would you not let God lighten your load, ease your earthly responsibilities?

"Habit?"

Can you be any more vague?

"Well, that's what comes to mind."

Here, let Me help you, Beloved.

You are having to work so hard because you still carry the feeling left over from your childhood that you are not good enough. You still think you must prove to others that you will come through in their times of need.

This is the kind of stuff that has blocked My Light from entering you. Hauling around these "having to do" burdens is why you still sometimes find yourself emotionally and physically exhausted. If you keep it up, it is your body that will pay in the end.

You must realize that you can serve Me in a far greater way than by trying to find love through approval. I need you, Loved One! Not to *find* love, but to *be* Love. This is your greatest responsibility. I promise that meeting it will be no burden on you and will benefit everyone. Until then, if you should ever feel overloaded, do the exercise you just learned. That will let you bring consciousness back into your heart.

Dearest, why wait to come to what you call "terms" with any aspect of your life? Why not let your heart's Rapid Response Team do the healing now?

"I guess my attempts to heal the present haven't worked because I'm so used to living from past to future."

No wonder. With your current way of looking at things, cause, *then* effect, is how you think it goes. But, though you perceive the past and future to be completely different, I do not. In actuality, they are two sides of the same coin. Cause implies a past intention when measured against effect—the manifestation of that intention over a linear period. Thus, past and future have no choice but to be bridged by the eternal now, the wormhole that folds time and space. Believe Me, the moment you launch an intention, it is manifested!

As long as humanity is lost in time, all manifestations will seem to come as future occurrences. But as you release more fear, the time it takes for you to notice such manifestations will quicken. Only when you remove all doubt and mind clutter will you begin to assume mastership and be able to both manifest what you desire in a holy instant and anchor the Divine Principles for life.

"Does time have any benefits?"

Right now, the buffer of time is of great benefit to you, for if it were not for this shock absorber, the fear encapsulated in your head could not handle events that might manifest immediately. Can you see why, in the afterlife, this is referred to as hell?

"Yes I can, because we exist in Spirit form there and cannot use time to act as our thought-buffer."

My, you catch on quickly! It is time that has fooled you into not knowing that you create your entire existence. The difference between you and Me is that you have been caught up in its illusion and bound to the body, so you cannot possibly see the next reality you have already created. Why? Your ever-active fear has denied you clarity and Self-love.

"Will You tell me more about what hell actually is?"

Yes, but I shall do that as we go along. For now, let us stick to the subject at hand.

When you unify with God, you become a part of something so divinely laid out that struggle ceases to be an issue. You have only to think something and—bang!—it happens. This should give you some idea of the inexhaustible Love I have for you.

Many people remain unaware of how to create deliberately. But now that you are learning how, Beloved, you can choose to not react to circumstance, but instead, put the power of Love into action to bring about what you desire and deserve.

Everything is there for you to understand, cultivate and grow from. Even so, to live "the good life," you must own every aspect of it. Only then can you begin to mend your personality that is split between pleasure and pain, good and bad, Love and fear. When you find your balance within the Divine dichotomy, your life will become one of Infinite Potential.

I ask you, has it not been rough living with this confusing split and not really knowing for certain who the heck you are?

"Oh God, yes! Sometimes it's been too much to bear."

In your earlier years, you tried to be a "good" Christian by ignoring your darker side; but this did not work for you because all your un-tended to fears were left to grow wild like weeds. When they got thick enough, they started to leech vital, nourishing energy that could have been used for your enlightened growth. Dearest, you have cut those weeds down quite a few times by doing productive things. But because you have not yanked all of them out by their roots, over time they have regenerated and have caused you even more grief. That is why the results they have produced have been neither permanent nor absolute.

Some of your fears are still mani-festering in your subconscious—inactive, but so very active. Because of your well-intentioned attempts, you sometimes think they are gone, but they are not. And as long as you continue to neglect them, the energy flow within you will continue to be obstructed.

Now do you think you know the answer to the question, "If I'm a good person, why do all these 'bad' things happen?"

"Yes."

Even so, I still see you and others pray to many deities when you are troubled. Sometimes you must wonder if your prayers are heard.

"Well, are they?"

Beloved, you know better than to ask that.

"Yeah, I do. But why is it that sometimes we don't get what we ask for?"

You always get what you ask for! No prayer remains unanswered, though sometimes it may seem to be that way. Even a prayer that comes from lack is answered and, since lack can only beget lack, if you ask Spirit to help you to be irresponsible, then so be it. If you expect any deity to unburden your troubled souls, you will all be waiting for a long time. Why should anyone other than you assume *your* responsibility?

"I don't know. Why?"

Because My system is not designed to work any other way. Because the Lord helps those who help themselves. Because Heaven on Earth cannot be anchored until everyone assumes My kind of responsibility!

Now is the time to assess your self/Self in a way that you have not done before. Believe Me, denial is not that river in Egypt. Denial only creates piles of confusion, kind of like the dog poop you inevitably step in because you do not see it. To help yourself out of the mess you are in, you must wear responsible shoes and walk responsibly in them. Responsibility only comes when you embrace your entire Self, fears and all.

"I wish I could just throw all my fears in the trash can."

If you could, along with that toss would go the wisdom that shapes you, for both are parts of your perfect design. And besides, if you did not have the fears you have, you would be someone else.

What you *can* do is change what fear means to you. See it as a tool to help unfold the wisdom you have within. You are the Dreamer, your own Creator Almighty; and yes, Keith, it is you who have been making this up for a very long time—in fact, for an eternity!

I am pleased to tell you that you are getting much better at the "making up" process. I see you manifesting reality with effortless ease in your sleep states of consciousness, and I know that your goal is to be able to do this in the waking world. But because of your repeated mistakes, you have been stuck in time—trapped between realms. The truth is, you are in perfect placement to get to the other side of stuck, which is freedom. You are close—so close!

"What do I do to keep getting closer?"

Again, call a meeting with the two aspects of your self/Self and have a healing session. Go inside and embrace your pain, invite it, feel it, then change what it means to you by recognizing from your heart's perspective the beauty of your predicament.

"What do You mean by 'the beauty of my predicament'?"

That I am with you every moment, just waiting to give you the gift of your True Self. Dear One, you must do as you have done before and ask, "God, where are You in the illusion that overwhelms me?" Then step outside of it and watch Me go to work on your situation. But stay aware of My every move so you will know when it is time for you to step back in.

It gives Me immense joy to be consciously recognized by you — the very same joy you get when you know that you are recognized by Me. This is how you anchor Me within you and come aboard the Good Ship Homeward Bound.

Keith, I see you as a slumbering aspect of Myself. So, as your Loving Parent, I say to you, "Hey, sleepyhead, are you not ready to get up and start your eternal day?" My Divine Child, awaken and use your God-given instincts as your guide. Your whole life awaits!

"What do You mean by instinct and where does it come from?"

Instinct is life's common thread of knowing and purpose. It comes from all previous times to guide you on the right path — the path to Spirit.

"I see."

It is not enough to see. You must look! "And ye shall seek Me, and find Me, when ye shall search for Me with all your heart." (Jeremiah 29:13–14)

To All My Children: For the world to attain Heaven on Earth, things cannot be as they are now. It will take all nationalities coming together to achieve the goal of love, peace and unity. Trust that I will guide you in whatever you do. Just remember to breathe and do your very best to live in Love, give in Love, be in Love — and Love you shall receive! It is time to embrace yourselves, embrace all of humanity and embrace the Earth. Do this and you embrace God. Join Me!

*As soon as you can
determine what to do
and what not to do
in any situation,
living a peaceful life
will become second nature.*

*Look for
the deepest meaning
in every reality.*

CLARITY

Are you beginning to see your healing process in action, My Friend?

"Yes, very much so!"

My aim, no matter what may be placed before you, is to always bring out the Divine in you. How you yourself choose to deal with your trials and tribulations is another matter entirely. As you get closer to the core of who you really are, the more clarity you have, the better you will be able to deal with anything.

Clarity

Clearness (in various senses).

The condition of being clean and free of contaminants.

Absolute clarity is one of My grandest attributes. For you to have it too will require crystal clear intention—a lifelong commitment of your spirit, mind and body—your feelings, thoughts and actions—constantly working to dislodge and discard all beliefs that block clarity's light. Every time you employ discipline and dedication, you will be getting closer to Me at a conscious level. I shall now show you an excellent way to begin this process.

When you awaken each morning, stay supine for a few moments. Go over the dreams you had while your body was at rest. As you start to interpret these mind movies, how you feel about them will let you know whether or not you are clear. Then you will know how to adjust your visualizations so you can intentfully plan the way you wish your day to go. Your clear intent and positive attitude will set the tone, and the day you desire will unfold.

Each evening just before you go to sleep, think about what did not align with your morning's visualizations and be grateful for all that did. Then ask for the clarity to fine-tune your prayers and intentions so that tomorrow will be a better day. As soon as you can determine what to do and what not to do in any situation, living a peaceful life will become second nature.

Keith, you have always had creative power. What has kept you from maximizing it has been your cluttered mind. Why not look at your creative process like this:

You are a movie projector and God is the Light inside. Your thoughts are the film itself. As you sit in the theater of life, what movie is playing on that 3D screen of yours? A horror flick? If so, change the film!

The simple fact is that, conscious of it or not, you are the producer and director of your own movie, and any sad or unfinished scene in it will only become more difficult to wrap if you do not take responsibility for its content.

Is your life playing out the way you want it to? If not, the only way to get it to go the way you truly desire is to do the work necessary and get clear about it. That is the crux of it—no more, no less. Neither good nor bad. Your life is the movie you make.

Do you sometimes get frustrated because things do not seem to work out the way you intended?

"Yeah, for a long time my life has been *filled* with frustration and confusion. Up until the last few years, I didn't know it all spawned from my intentions."

I will tell you this: You have gotten and are getting exactly what you have intended. With whatever degree of clarity you have had, you have intended. Even if someone does not make a choice, still a choice is made—the choice to remain complacent. Thus do the patterns of sameness evolve—by one's unaware intentions.

For those who accept and apply the wisdom of this simple truth, life will get easier and more fulfilling. For those who do not, trouble will remain. Either way, everyone will go on creating. And either way, you will all get what you want.

"Well then, what I want is enlightenment!"

If you truly wish to bring perpetual Love into your daily

life, becoming pure is imperative. Only then can Spirit lift you higher, so that the dive from your ego into Its Arms will be a graceful one. Once your clarification and elevation begin to accelerate, people will recognize that you are living with more joy. That will be your confirmation of the work you have been doing.

"Boy, I can't wait for that day to get here!"

Do not be in such a hurry, Keith! Where you are now is a normal part of the process. The goal is not the goal; the journey is. If you focus on the future, you will lose the power of the present moment.

"Why do I still find it so hard to tell the difference between what's Spirit and what's my ego?"

Every aspirant on a spiritual path goes through this phase of not being able to tell for sure when the ego is dominating. But your not knowing says it loud and clear —the ego is still in charge. Yes, even though knowing is your natural state, you still sometimes depend on your ego for answers it is incapable of providing. You see, since *the ego can never communicate with Spirit*, it will always insist that it is *you* who is the incapable one. When it does that, doubt begins to creep in and you stray away from being the deliberate creator that you so want to be.

I am advising you to relax now, Dear One, for Spirit will provide you with what the ego can not. Open, accept, be clear and know, and your life will speak for itself.

"But I still sometimes judge my lack of progress."

Ah, but the universe knows no lack! Believe it or not, what you may regard as lack is actually progress.

Everything always moves forward. Because *you* do not yet see evidence of this is evidence to Me that you are still in the progress process. Do not be so hard on yourself, Beloved. Give yourself some grace like I do.

Bit by bit—or by leaps and bounds—the clarity that comes to you will benefit not only you alone, but the people around you and in the world as well, all of whom can use as much healing as you will be able to offer.

————◆————

"Will You share with me some of the universe's mechanics?"

Through this book, as well as many others, it has been established that Love is all there is and there is nothing else. Now I will explain how the mechanisms of Love sustain the whole universal system.

The universe rests upon the Divine Principles of Clarity and Love, which form the light grid through which Spirit travels. These two principles allow the Divine to be omnipresent. The good news is that you can hitch a ride with Spirit if you elect to abstain from your earthly bad habits and make that abstinence part of your routine.

"Do I dare ask...um...what do You suggest I work on?"

For starters, change your diet by eating less and by staying away from fast foods and cured meats. Include more fresh fruits and vegetables in your menus. Before long, you will be amazed at the added energy you have.

Besides being prone to eating poorly, you have taken on other bad habits along the way, dabbling in lots of things from the outside world that have provided you with quick thrills. But they have not satisfied you, because if they had, you would not have returned for a second (and third and fourth...) helping. Even now, any time you want some immediate gratification, your mind is more than willing to remind you of all the things that will give it to you. With cigarettes for example, you smoke one after another because the mind has you convinced that doing so will bring you some satisfaction.

All addictions hamper growth because of the useless mind noise they create — a noise so loud that Spirit's whisper gets lost in the din. Sad to say your vices will stick around until you find the clarity (mind silence) that will let you listen to Spirit.

"What about what addictions do to the body?"

Understand that the mind and body are not separate, for in the empty space of body is mind. Actually, the body is the mind solidified. So if one part of the mind is ill (not clear), over time, what that part demands will begin to poison the body. And, over time, you will actually be able to observe your body manifest mind or Spirit, whichever one you have chosen to let govern your life.

The addictions I speak of here are the ones that affect people the most — cigarettes, drugs, alcohol, food, gambling and sex.

"But are we not allowed to experience those things?"

Yes, if you choose to. But problems set in when you *have to* have it, not when you are occasionally indulging in something simply to enhance your fun. But do not be fooled by the "I'm not an addict; I do it because I like doing it" tricks that the mind likes to play on you. You know where you stand, Keith. If you find that your addictions are getting the better of you, know that you have lost sight of your goal of Self-fulfillment.

"From now on, when my mind tells me I need something, I'll try to pay more attention to what's really going on."

That would be good to do because every unhealthy habit or addiction you keep hold of only affirms that you intend to stay within the limits of earthbound reality. With each attempt to give up these vices, you take another step towards the clarity that will finally let your Higher Self settle into place.

Beloved, I tell you yet again that there is so much abundance within you. But how can you expect to see that when you are not yet clear?

"So You're telling me that the reason I've stayed so frustrated is because I haven't been able to realize Your Bounty and to manifest it? Is that it?"

Not only that. Your frustration has thrown your mind into ego overdrive and that, combined with your feelings of need, makes you think that you must "get it while the getting is good."

"Isn't this the way the world operates?"

Not entirely, but you are correct in one sense. There are many lack-minded corporations that refuse to let go of their need and greed to possess and monopolize. They are the primary reason the Earth's health has gotten so poor. If they are allowed to continue, their ongoing abuse of the planet will hasten her dying and death.

"What can we do to keep that from happening?"

The clearer everyone gets, the more effective you will become at removing their parasitic energy because you will be using your own God-given power to correct the seemingly irreversible damage they have done.

Everyone must change from poverty thinking to prosperity thinking. When that happens, you will each become a channel for abundance to return, radiate outward and help heal the planet. Once everyone looks upon Me as the Infinite Repository of Wisdom and Wealth, the world's spiritual revolution/resolution/evolution will begin and lack will end.

"You mean there'll be no more starving people in the world?"

No, I mean you will no longer see these people as starving, but as nourished. It is this very shift in perception that will compel you to do what is next in sequential order — feed the world.

"So what You're saying is that there is no lack of anything anywhere?"

Lack is your point of view, My Friend, not Mine, and that point of view is the cause of all your quandaries. Why the world has not addressed the hunger problem more aggressively baffles Me!

"Have we insulted You?"

What "insults" Me is that you have done so little with all I have given you.

"But what about all those organizations that feed the

hungry?"

Are there still starving people in the world?

"Yes."

Then you have done nothing but *attempt* to feed the hungry. Because the world still operates from lack, it thinks that enough is being done, but that belief only keeps you worshipping the almighty dollar instead of the Almighty within that can provide the world with everything it needs.

"From what You've said so far, it sounds to me as if we have to die before we can go through this spiritual transition. Is this true?"

No, that is not the case at all. But many are so caught up in their life's drama that all they know themselves to be must die in order for love, trust and clarity to be born —in order that they may live.

I am pleased to say that you are dying gracefully, Keith. And as long as you continue helping others and keep striving for clarity, you will one day be able to tap into the power that will let you manifest a body to live in whenever you want.

Look around. Can you see how everyone must come to clarity before the chaos can be dissipated?

"Clearly."

The more of you that take part in this process, the more you will be able to influence the time/space coordinate of your ascension. Yes, as many of you as possible must work through your chaotic energy because, if you continue to feed your addictions, you will deprive yourselves of Me, and your fear and confusion will be all that remain.

"Why is peace so difficult for us to get to?"

Many do not know what peace looks like because they make no effort at all to familiarize themselves with it. It cannot be said enough: *It takes love, trust and clarity to live the peace that lies within you.*

This is your moment, My Child. For lifetime after lifetime I have watched you work diligently so that you could be here now, preparing for this grandest time in history. Do not take this life for granted, lucky one, because there are many souls who still await the chance you have been given —human birth!

———◆·———

Clarity and Love are the building blocks that give the universe its form and maintain its integrity. They are the code and law you must follow to become aware of Spirit's omniscience—a reality that is only accessible to those who are no longer within shouting (or whispering) distance of the ego's voice.

Infinite possibilities reside within you now, Beloved. Can you see them? Can you hear them? Can you feel them?

"I see, hear and feel much, but throughout it all, I still get confused."

You will be glad to know that whenever you get confused there is a way for you to become clear.

"Really? How?"

By doing just that. *By asking Me!* The clarity you seek will come through when you repeatedly think of God and invoke My Name whenever you have concerns.

"Now I understand why I haven't been able to reach those higher realities as often as I'd like — it's because I'm still not completely clear. Did Jesus, Buddha and other deities go through this same process of purification that I'm going through?"

Yes, they did. Everyone must go through this process before their Light can fully emerge.

Beloved, you have already observed your own clarity in action because every time your knowing process has broken through it has given you quick glimpses of your life's potential. You were usually not able to make much sense of these images, but the deepest part of you knew that all was in order.

"Yeah, that's happened to me several times — when I've been able to flash on what seemed to be my future. And You're right, I somehow knew that my life was surely going there."

Remember how tough it was to put that feeling into words?

"Yes, why's that?"

Because the experience was yours alone. Whenever you have such an experience (and this goes for life in general), what you must try to do is remove your beliefs from what you think is happening. Take care not to ground yourself in what you think is going on, because that will only lock it in. Toss the images around as much as you must — and I invite you to do so — but know that any restrictions such as your beliefs (fears) will only inhibit you and keep you in a state of non-elevation.

"One night years ago, when I was asleep, I had an incredible spiritual experience that filled me with utter bliss. Did it mean that, for a moment at least, I was without belief?"

Yes, Dear One, in that one glimpse, you did touch an aspect of your Soul. But though you have had those few moments that felt like nirvana, never claim that you have finally found Me, for this will only block you. Instead, continue to look for the deepest meaning in every reality. As you do, you will notice a powerful shift in your thoughts and feelings, a shift that will let you feel even more of that Higher Self ecstasy when you are awake.

"Yes, after that experience I felt so intuitive!"

Did you find that your mind was more frequently filled with thoughts that somehow did not seem to belong to you? And is this not what you are now experiencing with the writing of this information? Dear One, you are beginning to unify with the Mind of One where no one owns thought but Me. You have been growing your omniscient (psychic) gift all this time so that we can communicate telepathically now. Do you not agree that life is getting somewhat easier?

"Much!"

Making contact as you did and listening to guidance as you do has taken miles off your journey Homeward. But you must be careful not to become euphoric over the idea that *everything* you hear is guidance when you make these kinds of psychic shifts. You must be careful not to let the ego reinstate itself into your decision-making.

You may ask how to discern between the guidance and the thoughts that you wish were true and how to keep yourself from falling into this mighty trap of uncertainty again and again.

"Help!"

There, there, My Child, it will be all right. Your goal should be to keep it simple, because your frustration when you do not will cancel any headway you may have made. In times of uncertainty, show gratitude for the clarity you already have and call upon Spirit with all your heart to help you dissolve your doubt. I touched on this earlier in the chapter and now I will expand on what I have already said.

Ask yourself this important question: Is this true guidance or just something my ego is projecting? If you are asking such a question in the first place, you have already gotten your answer from Spirit—whatever it is, is not Spirit!

"Are You saying that what I wish were true and true guidance can never be the same?"

I am not implying that guidance will not lead you to what you want. What I am saying is that as you work to develop your psychic gifts, the ego will be working just as hard to convince you that *its* voice is the voice of guidance and the only one you should be listening to. That darned ego will always try to throw a monkey wrench into the ol' Keith-machine, hoping to keep you from your happiness. So pay close attention to who is doing the talking!

"No wonder it sometimes feels like I'm losing my mind."

Oh how I hope so, Dear One!

"What the . . . ?"

I shall explain.

Your mind is the root of all your blocks and problems. It contains way too much stuff that serves no purpose whatsoever. So you must lose your mind—purge it thoroughly—until what you know as mind is lost.

Since you are just beginning your omniscient development, I know this may be confusing for you. But if you are patient and persevere in your spiritual practice, all will blossom in its proper season. Just continue to be on the lookout for synchronicity in your life, for it will let you know for sure when your guides are the ones seeking your attention.

And, Keith, remember that growing your psychic abilities is not the goal. The goal is God, God, God! The abilities I grant are My gift to you so that, in time, they can become a powerful tool for your work. I want you to know I have complete faith that you *will* pull through this transition.

———•———

It is not the practices, props and other superstitions everyone has been accustomed to when worshipping that will lift you all towards conscious union; it is your sincerity. And believe it or not, as you develop your levels of spiritual mastery, you will no longer even need to pray.

"How could that possibly be?"

Up until now, you have had to depend on prayer

because your own Divine forces have been latent. However, when you have your own Love power, you will have the Will to accomplish for yourselves what you have always called upon Me to do.

Continue to use the rituals that you are familiar with if they help you to fall deeper into a meditative state; and if it helps you to stay humble, then by all means pray! Keith, I assure you that your need for these rituals will one day disappear. Meanwhile, just continue being sincere, for that is what will hasten the your ego's demise.

"This may be off point, but can You tell me if there are benefits to being alive now rather than in earlier times?"

Yes, you have it much easier now. Those before you who sought enlightenment did not have one benefit you have: the readily accessible collective power of the awakening many. That power, properly channeled, can propel all of you right into the Divine.

The ones who reached enlightenment long ago had to overcome by themselves the pull of many dark forces — but they did it. Yes, Great Ones such as Moses, Buddha and Christ lit the Divine Lamp of Love to illuminate the path for you.

Each time Teachers such as these achieved an advanced state of omniscience, omnipotence and omnipresence, a potent burst of energy was released upon the lower strata. If you study Scripture, you will see that it points to yet other Divine comings, indicating that Teachers of this magnitude have not finished visiting Earth.

One such coming, Bhagavan Sri Sathya Sai Baba, has

attracted millions to bear witness. They have come to South India from all around the world to see Me, hear Me, feel Me and know Me through this Avatar (Divine Descent)—to see evidence of My Love and Grace in this human incarnation.

When these pilgrims return home from India, the brilliant burst of Light they were saturated with affects others, whether or not they share stories of the miracles they beheld. Thus Sai Baba's beam is able to radiate far beyond His physical location. Even so, many people will question the existence of this Avatar, to say nothing of His work and some of the things that take place around Him. From the western point of view, the very idea of this particular embodiment of Mine will be seen by many as nothing but wrong.

"My own experience sure helps me to understand how that could happen."

When you (or anyone who has seen Sai Baba for him/herself) tell people that this Avatar creates objects out of thin air and is able to resurrect people...well, you tell Me, Keith, how *do* they respond?

"They usually react with fear and disbelief."

Yet, after hearing of My arrival from others, many have gone to the ashram in India to observe with their own eyes what Sai Baba is up to. Some go with unaware intentions and have learned valuable lessons. These lessons I provide without judgment and in all Love. Some of these curious ones return home to share Sai Baba tales that are good and some return to tell ones that are not so good.

But those who go and then question Sai Baba's authenticity do not understand the mission of this Avatar. Or, perhaps, they are simply not yet willing to believe that what is happening is really happening and is for their betterment—for *God's* sake.

Let Me say here that all suspicions about My incarnation as Sai Baba are good, for questioning encourages the search for answers. And let Me further say that there is a reason for everything that takes place at the ashram. That reason is to help everyone there to complete past karma and to find Me within themselves so that they will no longer worship God as another! There is no other reason.

"I've been to the ashram and my experience was completely divine! I was able to touch my Soul while I was there and for that I will always be grateful."

You have such good things to say about your trip to Sai Baba, Beloved, because, for the most part, your karma is good. And it is for this very same reason that I have selected you as one of My scribes. Those with less commendatory stories are just on a different path.

"Thank You so much for helping me understand that part of Sai Baba's mission is to help others see who they really are, even at the expense of His own reputation. What an unselfish act!"

You are welcome!

Later on, I shall speak of yet another Divine incarnation that will come to the continent of America.

"Wow! I'll be looking forward to that."

It is because of incarnations such as Sathya Sai Baba that

the world can be lifted out of darkness and human elevation can be made possible. Yes, Dear Ones, since you are
no different from these Masters, not only is it possible for
each of you to reach their level in your lifetime, it is your
duty.

But do not be fooled into thinking that all you need to
do is process a little here and a little there, and — Boom!
— you are God. Granted, your pure and genuine intent is
important, but there is much to iron out before you can
become God-conscious. For example, you must still work
on the karmic patterns from both your past lives and your
current life's past. You do that by doing what I recommend, by expanding the Love within you until you
consciously reach the level that *is* God. To reduce the risk
of moving backwards, you must always "keep on truckin',"
knowing that I walk beside you and you never again have
to be afraid.

Keith, I see you wanting to get higher but as the many
aspects of your life are becoming finalized, I also observe
the fear that is causing you to resist the changes that are
taking place. My Son, change is inevitable! Just wait and
see — the more you close the old doors of your life, the
more new ones will open for you.

"So, how do I get comfortable enough, despite my fears,
to walk confidently through them?"

All you can do is prepare yourself for what may lie
ahead. The clearer you become by doing Self-work, the
fewer fears will crop up and, no matter what door you find
yourself approaching, you will begin to recognize it for the

opportunity it is. Indeed, as the path you are seeking begins to announce itself with more and more certainty, you will not feel comfortable *unless* you walk it. You already know this! This search you have embarked upon pulls at your heartstrings. It nudges you to keep moving towards God's Peace.

"But what if it turns out that I'm not on the right path?"

This is a common worry for most spiritual aspirants. But the truth is that no one can ever get off the path that is meant for him or her. If someone feels that they have strayed, this concern of theirs will put them right back on it.

Here is the path: Just stay in the present moment at all times. It is this awareness of the now that will keep you from being caught off guard by events that, in the past, would have caused you to react. It is not accurate to think that you can deviate from your life's design. The fact is that *not recognizing the path is actually part of your path.*

No matter what road you take, your life is in My Hands. But when you worry and try to control your life, it is as if you are trying to yank it out of My Hands — insinuating that I cannot do the job well enough. If that is your position, I assure you there will come a day when you will wish that you had trusted Me (Higher Self) from the very beginning.

"But it's such a challenge for me to let go of my wants."

You are not alone. There are many that think they know what will give them peace. But yet, even when they get what they think will do it, it turns out that peace is not a permanent part of the package. Tell Me, Keith, why do you think peace is so difficult for people to reach?

"Because somehow all our wanting has managed to divert us away from You."

You have listened well. Have there not been times when you tried and tried to get what you wanted until you were utterly frustrated?

"Yeah. I would get tired of trying and say, 'Ah, forget it!'"

And how many times have you thought that what you wanted was never going to show up, only to hear Me say, "Here it is!"? You see, peace was there for you all along, but until you decided to release your self-inflicted burden of want, all you got for your efforts was a stressed mind, emotional conflict and physical exhaustion. For what reason? Beats Me!

I speak now to all My Children: What you must understand before you can fulfill your passions is the difference between wants and desires. I know this may sound contradictory, but it is not, because wants are "having to have" energies and desires are "God, You are my peace and if it is Your Will, this would be nice" energies. When you believe the former will bring you peace, rather than God who is Peace Itself, you negate any chance that your desires will be fulfilled.

When you choose God as the primary force and focus in your life, all things move toward you, not only because of the magnetic light you radiate, but because, within God, all things exist. As soon as you allow Me to take up full-time residence in both your mind and your heart, you will flourish.

———•———

Now to true faith. When you achieve absolute clarity, you will have it. And along with it will come all the power you need to manifest an ideal life. Faith, Clarity and Power: three facets of My Loom of Life, working together to weave all of Creation. These three cannot be separated lest all cease to be. Their immutable threads spin a tapestry of conscious awareness that becomes a Divine Garment for all to don.

Do you see the glorious pattern I am constructing here?

"I think You're talking about unity."

Yes, the mighty power of all working together to benefit the All to bring about change. It should not be hard for anyone to see that two is mightier than one, three mightier than two, four mightier than three — to the Infinity that is God — One.

Faith not only describes belief in a particular religion, it also conveys one's hope for a particular outcome. Those who assume that results will come through blind faith cannot see how the power to manifest only springs from absolute knowing. Yet they are willing to gamble that their expectations will pay off — that they will hit life's jackpot — without realizing that they have nothing at all to back up their bet.

A believer *hopes* that his or her life will happen; a knower *makes* it happen by having the faith-supported gumption to go about living it. For some, their belief can be a crutch for laziness. But if you want it to, belief can easily become the catalyst to expand you into absolute knowing.

Faith can also be applied to the principle of believing in something higher than you. This is but a metaphor because *there is nothing higher than you.* Many will say, "But this sounds like blasphemy!" I know that pondering such a thought may frighten many and may put religious leaders in a state of God-panic. So to them, I ask: How can such a beautiful thought about the Divine nature of all generate such fear?

"Well, haven't many religions taught that we are less than the Divine beings?"

Just because they say you are inferior does not mean that you are, for I have created no one above or below another. I do not separate nor favor anything, nor am I for or opposed to anything. If I operated this way, I would not be the Unity that I am. To clear up this long-held misconception is the purpose of our transcription, Beloved. That is: to help you to see all things through the eyes of Love.

"So what's it like to see and to be in this supreme state?"

Simply divine! So crystal clear is My vision that everywhere I look, all I see is Me! I am not *the* supreme being. I *am* Supreme Being, and My Beingness permeates everything in creation like light moving through glass.

"Is everything crystalline in structure?"

Yes, exactly. From My Mind, all information passes through fiber-optic light branches to manifest everything everywhere all at once—illuminating Me as the Source of All that Is. By purifying that within you which remains clouded and constricted by fear, you, too, will come to see and be in this state.

"What a great session this was for me! I do believe I have much more clarity now."

I am very pleased to hear that, Keith, because if this chapter about clarity provided none, what would have been the point?

Just remember:

> C all upon God in times of confusion.
> L ove is the power! Love is all there is.
> A llow and accept yourself and all people.
> R aise your vibrations by living My truths.
> I ntend to marry your God Self completely.
> T rust that all things will unfold accordingly,
>   according to ...
> Y ou. It is all about you! Where there is clarity,
>   there is peace.

There are always
more aspects of truth
to be revealed
and they come in ways
you cannot imagine.

The concept of victimization
does not, cannot
and will not
ever exist!

Fear of God?

I see that you have a question, Beloved. Write it down and I shall offer some insight.

"What have I really been seeking all this time?"

What you have been longing for is your own internal life fire. But because, until recently, you were "looking for love in all the wrong places," you have always fallen short of fulfillment. Your obsession with things external has taken over and left you feeling unguided and alone. Your belief in lack has driven your ego wants, urges and addictions. By overlooking the Spirit within yourself, you have been unable to fully realize that it is you alone who have held the key to your own bliss.

———— • ————

You have always been a walking question mark, My Friend. Now that you have sincerely asked for the truth, I shall gladly give you some answers.

Your whole life you have heard people opine that I am a hammer-wielding god who punishes anyone that dies with sin. Allow Me to clear this one up first.

Sin is not something that requires punishment. It is simply a miscalculation on your part that you must learn from and correct so that you can release yourself from the karma you have been bound to, so that you can put yourself back on track. You and many have bought into this concept, and since guilt is all you have known, you have remained in that mindset, all the while revering those who have achieved conscious perfection. The fact is that you could become just like them, but your fear, your feelings of inferiority and your sheer laziness have kept you from it.

Now, as you are eagerly learning about and from the "perfect ones" who preceded you, you see how much challenging work lies ahead, the concentrated effort you will need to exert in order to detach from worshipping the worldly things that most of you have grown accustomed to.

The perfect ones are not alone in their ability to accomplish such a state of consciousness. You yourselves, perfect-ones-in-waiting, can get there, too, by exercising your freewill to live righteously—choice by choice, thought by thought, feeling by feeling, deed by deed and day by day. If you keep on living the other way, you are merely passing time and keeping yourselves away from the Divine life that is rightfully yours.

"But I was taught that original sin is one of the things that stands between me and everlasting life."

It is not a sin to be born human, it is a privilege! But you can bet that the people who believe it is a sin are the same people who have no sense of the Self, who expect some kind of leniency from a judgmental god when they die.

My Children, you do not need Me to judge and punish you for what you do! You have already assumed that position yourselves — error by error, excuse by excuse, judgment by judgment, lifetime by lifetime.

I
Am
Here

to help all of you recognize the judgmental thoughts and feelings you have acted upon and the dreadful effects they have had on you.

On some level, you already know when you make a poor choice and you hold yourselves in contempt when you do. What many of you do not know is how to live a life *without* judgment. I can think of no better way to help you stop judging than to show you how.

First, let Me ask, why would I take anything away from you that you want and choose?

"You wouldn't, because that would violate our freewill."

Then, as I see it, what needs calibration is the way you see things. Almost everyone imposes right/wrong, good/bad limitations and because of them, you have created a god in *your* own image, contriving that I am judgmental like you, but a million times more so — or worse, as you would say.

You yourself know the inner conflict that comes when you live what you have been taught and believe to be true and are presented with the real truth and must decide how to handle it. When you regard Me as unconditional one moment and judgmental the next, no wonder you are all so confused.

"Yeah, it's no wonder I've questioned some religious precepts most of my life. They just don't make much sense to me, especially the one that proclaims that when I die, You will be there to judge me and that You will be judgmental in Your judgment."

But why would anyone not think they stand before Me *right now*?

"Maybe out of ignorance — from still thinking and believing God is out there and not here — or because we don't want to feel that we're responsible for our actions until the very day we die."

Know what? Both are true. Some do not yet understand the omnipresence of God. Others feel they can just keep buying time until that day, then deal with it then. But the deleterious effects of such self-judgment are happening here and now.

"But won't some people always believe that God will condemn them?"

Yes, but if they just take the time to meditate on that belief of theirs, their Soul will undoubtedly send them a message of assurance that I would do no such thing.

"Several times, when I've questioned the possibility of such punishment, I've been overcome by a feeling of reassurance and suddenly that punishment concept just didn't hold up."

There, you see, when you let Spirit in, it cannot! But for the many who cannot yet hear the Soul's message, life can be a never-ending mental tug-of-war.

"So what's their problem?"

They are still too wobbly. They keep on doing the back-and-forth mind dance, trying to figure out what to do about their troubles. That prevents them from being in the moment and in the stillness of God. If they would only take that brave dive into their hearts, they would be able to bypass their minds and eventually expose themselves to the unwavering truth that would make them solid as a rock. You see, truth needs no crutch, no explanation. Truth does not judge. It simply sits everywhere, waiting patiently to be recognized.

"It's still challenging for me not to use judgment."

When you find yourself judging, notice how it keeps you in separation mode, between what is right (good) and what is wrong (bad). And notice how it makes you want to turn away from what you see as the supposed evil. That is the relative mind at work, and a fear-based one it is! Goods, bads, rights and wrongs vary from person to person; yet each person arrogantly insists on basking in their rightness while they belittle others for their perceived wrongness.

"I've definitely been guilty of that!"

If the universe's foundation were built on judgment, it would be in the same pickle that many find themselves in on the earth plane. Indeed, if judgment were *My* modus operandi, anyone and anything not to My liking would be wiped out. People who believe in judging think that I will deal with them in the same way that they think they must deal with others. No wonder many have so little passion to be with Me. And I do not blame them. Who in the world would want to get next to a god that judges then condemns?

"I wouldn't!"

Neither would I!

But people who do believe that way find themselves in a Catch-22. That is, they love God and want to love Me more, but still they are afraid. Deep down, they sense that I am not judgmental, but what is stored in their gray matter tells them differently. They are confused about what to do and what not to do in their search for peace and fulfillment—in their search for God.

The fear and judgment that many of you harbor is undeniable evidence that you are still operating out of your heads, operating on what you believe to be true. It is this imprint that keeps you from knowing Me as Landlord of your heart.

"Sometimes I'm wobbly, too — I just can't decide what to do."

Am I correct in saying that each time you are confused it is because you are uncertain as to which choice holds the treasure you desire?

"You are so right."

Have you not figured out that that back-and-forth pressure is what creates those excruciating headaches of yours? Why do you do this to yourself?

"Good Lord, that's exactly what I keep asking myself!"

All that teeter-tottering and all you have to show for it are impermanent results, when what you are really trying to accomplish is a permanent fix.

Illogical as this may sound, the trick you must master is to raise your consciousness *down* from your mind and *up* to your heart. For it is there that no conflict exists, only the firm foundation on which you can build a more peaceful life.

To hone in on the heart, Keith, you must be aware of your ego and what it wants from you. Or rather, you must be cognizant of what you want from others—to take, not give—and be willing to change that.

Can you see how simply falling into the heart will benefit you? If you can do so, and I know you can, that permanent fix you have been searching for will be yours at last—a life of love for the rest of your days.

"When does the ego kick into gear?"

The ego is born when you are very young. From the time you are told "No!" repeatedly, you begin to separate from the grand scheme of things. As you continue to develop, the ego becomes more demanding, defining each of you, the children-turned-adolescents, as singular, separate. Your egos are thus set in stone.

"I understand, but can any of us escape it?"

Yes, but that poses quite a challenge because, with the familial/religious/governmental noise that runs rampant inside everyone's head, you are almost bound to be bound in judgment. That's why you feel so tied up! And to further compound the issue, some preachers teach that I am something other than you and thus misguide their flocks.

"I consider myself a Christian, and as beautiful as Christianity is to me, I get a weird feeling whenever I hear someone tell me that everything one needs to know about God is in the Bible. Is this true?"

What do *you* think?

"I think not. I don't think God can be compressed into fifteen hundred pages of *any* book. Besides, there are other books containing spiritual road maps from Masters of other religions who have incarnated all over the world throughout history."

Such a good answer! What people need to understand is that there is far more to Me than the ink, paper and concepts in any book. The truth is, I am more the *Energy* of any given book that purports to teach about Me.

"I'm pretty sure that's going to rub some folks the wrong way."

I care not at all about rubbing or being wrong. I am only interested in truth and its results. I say it is not wise for anyone to live his or her life by a book, including this one. One should search for the Truth (God) wherever one must —under a rock if need be—for I am everywhere. All it takes to find Me is the desire to do so.

"Are all scriptural books filled with truth?"

Some are not as complete as others, but for the most part, yes. When you feel no fear in your mind and your body—when your heart sings—you will know you have found some Truth.

"I can honestly say that this has happened to me many times."

Then you have stumbled upon many truths, My Friend. And I urge you to keep stumbling.

"Am I correct in saying that since the Bible is based on truth, the prophecies foretold in Revelation are going to come true?"

Any prophecy in the Bible that has been and might be fulfilled (whether positive or negative) is not necessarily the vision of the prophet alone, but is shared by the many who believe it will come to pass. Yes, those who are locked into believing that a prophet is right form a mass conscious power that will support them in their convictions. This would be great if the particular vision they share has a positive outcome. But what about one with a negative outcome? Do you want the prophet to be right about that, too?

"No, I don't. So what do we all do about that?"

Stop believing that any prophet knew or knows more than you do. All they have seen is where you are likely to be at some point in time and space. Hear Me when I say that the God that lived or lives in them and has enabled them to see, is the same God that lives in you and enables you to see differently.

"I've had some people tell me, 'If you mess around with the supernatural, you are doing the devil's work.'"

Well then, I guess that makes Me the devil, because

everything about Me is supernatural, is it not?

"Completely. I'm just saying that that's just one of the crazy things I hear from time to time from people who claim they know Scripture. It makes me want to ask — do You encourage the reading of any particular holy book?"

I say read as many as you can, My Friend. Why not be well rounded? If you are seeking God, why not jump into the hunt with everything you have? But simply reading is not enough, for what good does reading spiritual writings such as this one do you if you do not experience what you have read about? Whoever remains a dabbler will never believe that My Reality is obtainable.

"Can I share something really cool that happened to me?"

But of course.

"I stopped going to church years ago because of all the fear-filled preaching I was hearing. But a few weeks ago I began playing music at some Sunday services and I got really inspired by what I heard. Each time I left, I couldn't wait to go back and join with others like me who want (and are getting) the God of Love there."

Nice, is it not?

"Very, because I could never relate to that heavy devil stuff before."

That is why one should be selective about where one goes for spiritual sustenance. You see, there are some clergy who will never change their views about this subject.

"Why's that?"

Because the way they perceive God is the way they are most comfortable with, and they do not want to go through all the stuff they would have to do to come to another conclusion. These kinds of preachers can be harmful to one's growth, especially that of young people. If you see children or adolescents at a church where such a one preaches, it is likely they were dragged there, or at least were resistant to the idea of going. This is because, in their innocence, it hurts them when they hear anything such as "God is vengeful—God is jealous—God is judgmental—You are going to forever burn in hell when you die if you do something wrong!" But still, they are forced to listen to the separation and punishment proselytizing until they too become hypnotized and join the rest of the congregation in spiritual bereftness.

There is no other way to say it: Many churches have become Petrie dishes where the meta-culture of fear is grown and disseminated. Thus, generation after generation, the fear of God has spread like a virus through everyone in these congregations, and that has resulted in ongoing separation and judgment.

But even in churches where ministers teach unity with God, there are some in the assembly who have not yet accepted such a concept. Yes, it can be tough for My Truth ministers to undo the separation imprint that has been pounded into these people's heads for years.

As long as people remain in such a powerless and power-sapping mindset, imploring a deity to remove their problems will do them no good whatsoever. As I have said before, spiritual beings are ready and willing to help everyone, but when you pray with no self-responsibility, you can expect the supplication to be denied.

I can tell you that spiritual masters will not take on your responsibilities. What they will do is help you to become divinely empowered by moving you through the feeling that you are weak and inferior to their achievements. They burn with the passion to ignite the Holy Fire within all of you so that you can be God with them. This is not blasphemy. This is the Truth! *And the truth shall set you free!*

"Please tell me what You mean by 'the truth.'"

That you are God! Once you believe this, you have the key to your own freedom. Any fear of God you have is a fear of your own Self and that fear will exist as long as you see yourself as separate from Me.

I have just shared with you the ultimate secret that many have sought the answer to throughout the ages. The question is, from this point forward, what will you do with it?

"I'll integrate Your 'secret' until I become fully conscious of it."

Good idea, Keith. Are you ready to go for it?

"Like I said, ready and willing!"

So you understand My point that your fear has been a mirror reflecting your spiritual status?

"Yes! I've lived Your point and know it all too well!"

Then let Me ask you this: At this moment, now that you are beginning to connect consciously with Me, what is showing up in your life?

"Much more grace, joy, love and prosperity than before and many opportunities to live blissfully."

Then do you think you are finally allowing yourself to really live now?

"Yes, at least that's what it feels like."

You have indeed come a long way, because there was a time in your life when you were so sure that the world would be a tough place for you to be in. Once you stepped into it, you stepped into a reality that was based on your own ideas. You had already determined how the world was going to be—and so it was. Everything you believed was going to happen happened.

Your fright/fight/flight response seemed to be appropriate for your security and survival back then because you felt you needed some sort of refuge to fall back on. But such a posture created lessons and karma that had to be transcended before you could get on with your spiritual growth.

Now you and everyone else have come to the time when fear can be released for its ultimate expansion into Love. By living in the present moment and letting go of how you think things are, by always being aware of what dynamic is moving within you and by responding to everything around you with a loving attitude, you can all come to realize peace.

You already know the path, My Friends. Just continue to walk it so that you can one day celebrate that you and I are One! Christ said "I and My Father are One." (John 10:30) "The Kingdom of God cometh not with observation." (Luke 17:20) And He goes on to tell you exactly where it is: "Neither shall they say, Lo here or, lo there! For, behold, the Kingdom of God is within you." (Luke 17:21)

I implore everyone to search not for Me in the clouds, in the storybook place called Heaven, but in the part of your Self that is beyond time, beyond books and beyond words.

———•———

How are you today, My Friend?

"I'm good, but I have a question."

Please.

"Do You support any particular cause or religion?"

Yes, I do.

"Which cause, which religion?"

Love is My Cause and I do it religiously!

"Nice. I like that."

I am not an ambassador for any religion, creed, code or sect. I am much more than that. I help all of you to become better—be you Christian, Buddhist, Muslim, Jew or whatever.

"I'm so grateful to know of Your love for such spiritual diversity."

That is the way I envisioned the world to be when I created it. I am amazed that people do not recognize how their religions sing the same Love song to Me, albeit with different words. You are a musician, Keith. You know it gets old pretty quickly when you have to listen to the same song over and over.

"You have no idea! On second thought, yes You do. (laughing)

It does not matter where or how you praise Me because, to be perfectly honest, I do not need nor do I want your praise. What I "want" (if there is such a thing) is for you to cherish your *own* divinity, for that is what will bring about the very enfoldment and unfoldment of Heaven within you.

"Many preachers would disagree."

Yes, there are those who judge the ones who teach this way as being cultic or satanic, all the while claiming to possess the truth themselves. But I repeat, if it preaches separation, a church is not feeding its flock the Soul food it needs to flourish. It is not religion that is doing harm; it is the teaching of separation that does the damage. Any religious faith is valid as long as it does not extinguish the Fire of Unity.

One more thing. People call church the Lord's house, but this is not so. God does not dwell in a church if you are not there. *God dwells within you wherever you are.*

"So *I'm* the church?

Now you have it! Ideally, your church represents you — a solid structure and a True Temple of God.

"Man, oh, man . . . "

What?

"I just keep thinking of how some may respond to this book."

I know you are concerned that some may read and question it, then run straight to their religious leaders for answers. I wholeheartedly recommend this.

"Why's that?"

Because if someone attends a church that advocates fear and separation, he/she can then see for him/herself what he or she is a part of. People have the right to question any church's motives if "Everything is God" is not its mission statement.

Some clergy may attempt to convince their questioners that this book is a false testament and then try to reinforce the idea that God is something to fear. To them, I entreat: How can an unconditional God be the icon of fear? For I am Love in its Totality—complete unto Myself—afraid of nothing, extending Love and Grace from Myself to all for All.

"I so love hearing You describe Yourself this way."

Dear One, I am pleased that you have done the work that enables you to hear My Voice, unlike many who remain smothered by fear and, therefore, deaf to It. The purpose of this book, as well as others that have or will come out, is to help teach the "hearing-impaired" that I am not a vengeful god.

Some churches, even the one you were raised in, have painted a picture of what they believe Me to be. And up until recently, you yourself clung to and believed what you learned early on, thus making it true for you. You now know that everything you were taught "ain't necessarily so."

"No, it sure ain't!"

You are beginning to see there are always more aspects of truth to be revealed, and they come in ways you cannot imagine.

"You got that right. It seems like truth shows up when I least expect it. Why is it so elusive?"

To keep you *out* of systematic belief and *in* expansion mode. Want to know how to get to it? Open your mind. Open your heart. Continue to open yourself up to Me and trust that you are a part of All that is. Trust in your own ability to create a joyous, abundant life. Trust God in you, for I have given you your precious life and the very air you breathe.

Your daunting task now is to move through what has brought about your confusion, chaos and sickness—guilt, anger and fear—for the longer they stick around, the longer your conscious connection to the Soul will remain severed. Your freewill creates your life and, as you are created in My Image, your reality is certain to manifest!

———◆———

"Will You tell me a little about telepathy?"

You, Dearest One, were once quite telepathic. Now, as you write our book, you have begun to recover this ability. Indeed, not only you, but everyone, used to be in a conscious state of omniscience until the time when you left Home.

"What happened?"

Telepathic amnesia was spread by those that fell from Grace—the ones who became tainted at the time you all left the Godhead. These "do-no-gooders," with their distorted *modus operandi*, created mental blocks in an effort to obscure their selfishness. So universal law put their telepathy on hold and, as a fail-safe mechanism, the telepathy of those they affected as well. It was then that fear's domino effect kicked in, causing everyone to tumble faster, harder, until mistrust reigned. Such a powerful blow you took to your collective spiritual head that, for eons after, those who came to Earth could not remember their innate ability to communicate in this way.

Eventually, to reach each other from this lowered state, people had no recourse but to turn to speech. But, since human language is so limited, without telepathy there was much that could not be conveyed. People were thus put in a distrustful position, wondering what lay in another's mind that he/she could not or would not express. The suspicions that were subsequently raised had a profound effect on all and set the stage for what you now know as victimization.

"This oughta be interesting."

Quite. Many attach much power to that v-word because they feel it justifies whatever mess they make for themselves. It has long been used to deny that *they* are the weavers of their own life's tapestry. But the concept of victimization does not, cannot and will not ever exist! As far as I am concerned, any such claim plunges lifelessly to the ground, just as the tainted ones did in the great fall. Here is some good advice: Omit this word from your vocabulary and your mind.

"What actually happens in a victimization scenario?"

It is very simple—two Souls make an agreement to act something out on the earth plane. Let Me illustrate.

Late one night, a woman goes to the store to buy a few things. She decides to park her car in a dimly lit area. Why there when there were many other options?

"I don't know, why?"

Because she is carrying out her part of the agreement.

When she is through shopping, she returns to her car where someone sneaks up behind her. A crime is committed, but is she a victim?

"She's a victim of that crime, isn't she?"

If she desires to manifest her God-like Self, she does not claim to be one. Furthermore, if she were fully aware of her God-like Self, she would not have been in that predicament in the first place. This event is her Soul's effort to help her take responsibility for what happens to her while she resides on Earth. Follow Me here, okay?

"Okay."

How many souls are there by her car?

"Two."

The fact that both their bodies arrived at the moment they did shows that these two souls were only keeping their agreement. So, in truth, there was no perpetrator, no victim, ergo, no crime. Just the lesson.

I remind you that just because one may not be aware of an agreement, it does not mean that he/she is not responsible for what takes place between him/her and others. In order for anyone to get to his/her own true power, they must transcend all blame and acknowledge that they can never be a victim of circumstance in anything!

Let Me say here that even though you yourself still have

work to do, Keith, you have come a long way in under-standing the truth about victimization—or should I say, no victimization—and have begun to see how putting this knowledge into practice can reverse the power dynamic within you.

"Thanks. It's so good to hear that I'm making progress."

From now on, when troublesome scenarios show up, you will be better able to avoid feeling victimized by what-ever happens.

My hope for you, indeed, not only for you, but for everyone—is that you will all lose any sense of victimiza-tion you may have and begin to live empowered lives.

I
Am
Here

for anyone who chooses to work through their deepest fears concerning Me.

I
Am
Here

to help anyone who wants to make the shift from victim to God.

"Wow, there's a lot of power in what You've just said! But there's another question floating around in my head that I just have to ask."

Go.

"What about our court system and its laws? Aren't those based on victimization situations?"

Yes they are. Though there are many people taking responsibility for the lives they lead, there are many others who cry "Victim!" and take their grievances to court. As if the courts are not filled with enough lawsuits for this and lawsuits for that! The entire system is almost at critical mass and if the situation continues as it is, it will overload, short-circuit and, ultimately, collapse. The whole thing will become inoperable, leaving Divine Law to rise out of the mayhem. Then people will have no choice but to take responsibility.

Even though there will be many who do so, there will still be those who decide to be infuriated at a system they believed in, went so far as to contribute to, and by whose dogma they have chosen to live.

"I guess I'm a hypocrite then because, even though I don't have a beef with the legal system, I've harbored resentment towards religion and government for a long time. But I'm workin' on it."

And that, My Friend, is what I have been talking about —taking responsibility. But the fact is that, even after reading what I have just imparted about your present legal system, many will still do the opposite and they will fall hard.

"Did many Souls fall from Grace long ago because they did the exact opposite of what You said?"

Yes. They are the ones who actually believed they could

thwart My Plan of Heaven on Earth. Today's "tempters" of Luciferian influence are counting on you to help them achieve that same futile goal. Though they may be few in numbers, their influence is mighty.

I

Am

Here

to help each of you get back your power. But you must remember that those rebellious ones who now infiltrate the earth plane are destined for a great fall and they would love to take everyone with them once more.

"Who do You mean when You say 'they' and why would they want to do such things?"

They are the ones who have only themselves in mind as they attempt to gain world power. They have no compunction about inundating the masses with their convoluted fictions because they want to convince all of you to stay in line.

"You can bet that's one line You won't find me standing in!"

Do not be so sure about that because, since your arrival on Earth this time, you have been consuming what they produce and have thus been playing exactly by their rules. It appears to Me that you have become the product of your own lack of control.

"Are You telling me that this is my karma?"

Let Me give it to you straight, Keith, for I know the

results My words will produce. I came to you specifically because you asked for My help with such heartfelt passion. It is not only *your* victim karma that needs to be resolved —it is everyone's. And one way you do that is to accept that those who play the control game are nothing but a reflection of you.

"So what's the object of their game?"

As it has always been, to keep you unempowered and dependent—to keep you believing that whatever they say is valid. What throws Me for a loop is how so many of you still tend to place your bets on people like the ones who stopped so many others in their tracks that wanted to make a positive difference by elevating you!

"You're so right! We have been playing right into their hands because we still accept what they say and do and we rarely question it."

That has gotten a little old, has it not?

"Yeah, it sure has."

Do you really think these few are interested in abandoning their want for power? Do you think they will humble themselves to the Divine this time around?

"Nope."

It is likely they will not. They will never allow you to know all that they know because they are propelled by their love of power, not by the power of Love. Why do you think this is so?

"Because that would level the playing field."

How right you are, My Friend! They are only willing to share the information that will let them reign for as long as they possibly can. But when the world finally transforms its fear of Me into passion, they will go away.

All the knowledge your mind and heart can hold
I shall give you!
When you abandon fear
and use Love as your gauge and destination,
then all things beneficial will naturally come.

KNOWLEDGE = POWER = FREEDOM = BLISS

You are getting all this attention because you are considered to be universal royalty.

In all the cosmos, no species except humans can attain God-realization in physical form.

CREATION VS. EVOLUTION

Earth is so beautiful—a precious jewel floating in space. Yet, there are many who do not appreciate this glorious planet, who continue to regard it as a place to plunder. Almost everything I created to maintain balance in your ecosystem is being polluted and destroyed by such people as these, and if they are allowed to continue, there will be little left that makes life worthwhile.

————— • ◆ • —————

The entire universe is in a constant state of change—this never changes! Yet within this paradox, there is something that is fixed, permanent and absolute—an Anchor that moors the universe's intention, order, direction and unfolding. That something is God—

The
Unchanging
Changer.

Because you have begun to do so much internal work, Keith, your perceptions are heightened, and right now it seems to you that there are more changes happening than ever before. The fact is that nothing has really changed except your level of awareness. Back before it developed, what never seemed to change was that nothing seemed to be going right in your life. But your new cognizance has altered that for you, has it not?

"Yep, it has, and I believe I'm really starting to make some sort of sense of this paradox thing."

Y'think? Well, My Friend, you are correct, because I can see with each passing day that you are spotting the synchronicity (coincidences) in your life and are beginning to freely interact with them.

"Wow! So where does synchronicity come from, how does it manifest and what does it mean?"

It is born out of My Essence in the causal realm. From there, it swirls through your mind into your feelings, aligning events around you on the earth plane. But coincidences have no significance other than to get your attention through higher means so that you can grasp the very alignment you are in. Because you are beginning to truly open your eyes and ears, you can hear the higher language and can at last see order in what has always appeared to be chaos.

"I can see the chaos and, every once in a while, I can see

the order. But it's still a little challenging for me to see order *in* the chaos."

Keep looking, Beloved, because chaos is like a snow globe whose contents may be shaken but whose shimmering flakes always settle back into order. So it is in the physical universe: though things may be shaken, they still find their place to settle. Now do you see how there is order even in chaos?

"Sorta."

Soon, My Friend, soon. As you continue to awaken, everything will come into even clearer view. The pace of change will quicken for you and synchronized phenomena will occur more frequently. The more you can successfully navigate using the compass of synchronicity, the more effective you will be as the captain of your own mastership. Then nothing will slip by you unmonitored and the wake of your past will be replaced with your own will power. This is how you will evolve.

———◆———

"How did Earth come into being? Did it happen by a simple wave of Your hand or did it take billions of years like the evolutionists say?"

Ah, we find ourselves again with a this-or-that scenario.

"Yes, but which one is the truth?"

Have you not been paying attention, Keith? Both are. You have seen where right-or-wrong scenarios have landed you before. When you try to make one of these theories truer than the other, when this or that theory must prevail, you put yourself in a quandary from which there is no escape.

Be assured that *I* do not operate with such a mindset. The fact is, I threw the big bang switch and everything that has happened in the universe since then has evolved from that. Had there been such questioning on My part, Creation would never have happened—*I* would never have happened!

"But why did You do it that way?"

What other way was there? As for why, well, for the pleasure of watching everything transform from its lower state into its highest order—that includes you.

"Are You saying that..."

That is what I am saying all right. The big bang and evolution were the means by which I created the physical universe including Earth. Perhaps once "experts" learn more, there will be no more debating about this or that, no more debating about Creation versus the big bang and evolution.

Again, I present definitions to target and clarify our objective. I will start with the definition of 'evolve' and offer more plays on the word.

Evolve

To unfold or unroll; to open and expand; to disentangle and exhibit clearly and satisfactorily; to develop; to educe. The animal soul sooner evolves itself to its full orb and extent than the human soul.

The principles which art involves, science alone
evolves. Not by any power evolved from man's
own resources, but by a Power which
descended from above.

Let us add a suffix to the word 'evolve' to see where it
takes us.

Evolution

One of a set of prescribed movements.
A process of Change in a certain direction:
UNFOLDING. The action or an instance of
forming and giving something off: EMISSION.
A process of continuous Change from a lower,
simpler, or worse to a higher, more complex,
or better state: GROWTH.

A process of gradual and relatively peaceful
social, political, and economic advance.
Something evolved. The process of working
out or developing. The historical development
of a biological group (as a race or species):
PHYLOGENY.

A theory that the various types of animals and
plants have their origin in other preexisting
types and that the distinguishable differences
are due to modifications in successive generations.

The extraction of a mathematical root. A
process in which the Whole Universe is a pro-

gression of interrelated phenomena. Evolution that according to some theories involves the appearance of new characters and qualities at complex levels of organization (as the cell or organism) which cannot be predicted solely from the study of less complex levels (as the atom or molecule) — compare CREATIVE EVOLUTION.

Evolution that is a creative product of a vital force rather than a spontaneous process explicable in terms of scientific laws — compare EMERGENT EVOLUTION.

Now, let us look at the suffix itself.

-tion

A suffix used to form nouns from verbs.
Meaning: a-ing or b-eing, as in relation.
Something, as in Creation.

This definition offers an insightful word picture. It indicates the active process by which something is created (noun) because of actions (verbs) being carried out.

For the purpose of our discussion, '-tion' represents evolution, that which occurs when something changes from one state of being into another state of Being. Because humanity is expanding its collective awareness, it is starting to spiritually evolve, thus becoming the manifestation of that very definition.

Let us look closely at the last part of the last definition: 'a-ing or b-eing, as in relation. Something in Creation.'

You are the being with a relationship to something in Creation (God). But, since you have not yet reached God Consciousness, your evolution process, by its very definition, must continue.

"And God said, Let the earth bring forth the living creature after his kind, cattle, and creeping thing, and beast of the earth after his kind: and it was so." (Genesis 1:24)

The trail of everything on Earth except human beings leads inexorably back to the planet's original seed ingredients—amino acids. Early on in the evolutionary timetable, creatures emerged from the earth as a part of its adapting biology. Among them were some early forms of man, My works in progress, so to speak. But humans did not evolve from them.

Human is My selected creation. Adam and Eve came directly from Me. They were *of* the earth but not *from* Earth. Major difference. "So God created man in His own image, in the image of God created He him; male and female created He them." (Genesis 1:27)

Adam was born of Earth's own flesh (dust). Humans came into being when I, your Father, impregnated Earth, your Mother, with a spark of the Divine. "And the Lord God formed man of the dust of the ground, and breathed into his nostrils the breath of life; and man became a living soul." (Genesis 2:7)

Another passage reads: "And God blessed them, and God said unto them, Be fruitful, and multiply, and *replen-*

ish the earth, and subdue it: and have dominion over the fish of the sea, and over the fowl of the air, and over every living thing that moveth upon the earth." (Genesis 1:28)

Have you picked up on the clue in this bit of Scripture?

"Well, for some reason, I felt compelled to italicize the word *'replenish'* as it came through."

Good, you got that there were some who came before. If Adam and Eve had been the first, I would have had them go out and *plenish* Earth—not *replenish* it. They did, however, usher in the era during which I descended and walked the earth as man and woman.

Adam and Eve were the first embodiments of God Consciousness. In their nakedness they had no fear or shame because they saw each other as two forms of the same Self. It was only after they made the choice to "separate" from their Creator that they became afraid and could no longer see how they were connected to each other or to God.

Though man is different from all else in creation, you still must rise above the "original sin" of separation. But because of that very connection to Me through Adam and Eve—because of your natural state of Divinity, you have a head start on the evolutionary path and thus in your quest to reach My State of Being.

"So what You're saying is that every 'thing' has been some 'thing' else before and that's how the universe got to be where it is now?"

Yes. Everything has unfolded through many stages since the beginning of time. But only those capable of becoming *involved* with their own growth can speed up their *evolution* towards the ultimate state of *Being*, thus completing the circle of life.

Big Bang

A theory in astronomy: the Universe originated billions of years ago in an explosion from a single point of nearly infinite energy density—compare STEADY STATE THEORY.

The cosmic explosion that marked the beginning of the Universe according to the big bang theory.

Keith, this stuff might be a little tricky for you to grasp right now, but I know you will make a stab at it. The paradox here is that the physical universe is still expanding, while, from My standpoint, the universe just is. Yes, the bang happened, but it was not so cut and dried as it appears to have been.

There will come a time when the big bang will be accepted as the starting point of the physical universe and evolution will be seen as the dynamic and ongoing dance by which all things evolve into higher forms. But it will not make any sense until you can completely remove the factors of time and space from the equation. Only then will you see how these two are interwoven and are parts of the same phenomenon.

———•◆•———

I remind you that the universal design is the same from Cosmic↔atomic and from God↔godlet. When I express Myself, things shift.

More so now than ever before, when shifts happen, leaders and followers, knowers and doubters, will all begin to take their places for the final act of Earth's grand play. Everyone's choices will become apparent because of the definite consequences they will have. And since My goal —rather than change changing you—is for you to *become the change itself,* what I say now should serve you well as we embark on a discussion of global issues. Here we go.

Right now, at the beginning of the 21st century, Mother Earth, like you, is going through her own transformation. Your cooperation can help her to become an evolved planet, and help humanity to become evolved as well. Exciting, is it not?

"Very much so!"

You already know what your role will be, Keith—to be one of the bearers of the Divine Torch that many can use on their own way to spiritual freedom.

"I understand and I'm ready. So are many others I know."

Good, because I am counting on everyone to help Me so that Christ Consciousness can reign in the world for a thousand years to come.

"What'll happen after that?"

I love your insatiable curiosity about everything, but for now, it is best that you stay in the present rather than concern yourself with what may or may not ever be. If you wish, you can write *that* book later, one about your ancient past and your potential futures all the way back to the stars.

"Sounds like fun! I have so many books I'd love to write."

Then we shall write them, Beloved. But I suggest we move along with this one because you will also love what I am going to talk about next.

"Great!"

As you all embrace and use Christ principles, a beautiful garment—a multi-hued, crystalline system made up of the Self's subtle energies—will enfold you. Once you become aware of it, this light vehicle (called the merkabah) will be at your disposal.

"What's its purpose?"

The merkabah is what masters have used and still use to transport themselves through the different dimensions of the Creator Mind. It has infinite functions and can morph into anything, for it is not bound by a particular bio-track or body type. The merkabah is absolutely amazing!

"Is there more?"

But of course.

"Then do tell!"

When you become a master, you too will be able to tune light frequencies in and out to create just what you desire or even travel through the universe to watch a star being born. As you are starting to realize, you have all sorts of power at your fingertips. Soon there will be no limits to what you can do.

When Jesus ascended from your world, He was fully

aware of His Light. Because both you and He were born human, His life should show you how it is possible for you to become one with God just as He did.

During His time on Earth, Jesus taught those around Him that death is not the end of one's journey; that everyone resides in Spirit and in Spirit He and they would forever remain. But He knew His words were not enough to convince His disciples of everlasting life. So, three days after His crucifixion, Jesus decided to help them work through their doubts. He appeared in Spirit so that what He spoke of—the Lord before them as the Light—they had no choice but to see.

But what appeared before them was not what they were accustomed to seeing. What they saw was His light body, not His body in physical form. As the Light, He spoke to them, saying, "Touch Me not; for I am not yet ascended to My Father, but go to My brethren, and say unto them, I ascend unto My Father, and your Father; and to My God, and your God." (John 20:17)

Jesus personified the same Christ energy that is now being woven around all who are choosing alignment. Your merkabahs are beginning to spin faster and faster, slowly unleashing twelve strands of encoded and activated DNA. Through such a process, power long dormant will soon be yours.

"How many of us are ready?"

Millions. Yes, many involved ones will achieve Divine status with complete Soul memory and wisdom intact. Their collective light will then be the beacon that calls to all those still lost in the sea of humanity, casting about in the fog of fear. And Earth is also generating light. She, too, is becoming a beacon for all the ships still adrift in the galactic sea.

"Something really interesting's coming up, isn't it?"

Yes, we are about to talk about a subject that I know you are deeply fascinated with. Go ahead, Keith, ask Me the question you have wanted answered for so long.

"Great! What I want to know is, do other life forms exist in the universe?"

You already know the answer to that, but if it will make you feel better to hear Me say it, yes. What makes you think you need to ask, Dear One, when I have seen you play with angels? You do believe angels exist, do you not?

"Well, yes, but I mean . . ."

They *are* in the universe, are they not?

"Okay, yes."

There is your answer. But I know angels were not what you were thinking of when you asked that question. You want to know if there are any alien life forms interacting with your planet.

"You're right. That's what everyone wants to know." (brimming with anticipation)

The answer here too is yes. Do you not remember when you were a child and you woke in the wee hours of the morning to find yourself coming through the window, back into your bedroom?

"Yes, I remember that very clearly."

Remember how you could never recall going out the

window?

"Right."

Did you think you were sleepwalking or just roaming around the neighborhood because you were bored?

"I wasn't sure, but I've always suspected that I wasn't alone."

Your intuition was correct, My Friend. Deep within, you always knew.

"Yes, I guess I did."

What you were doing was connecting with other galactic life forms in a way that enabled you both to learn.

"But why was I selected to learn from them — and them from me?"

Because of an agreement you made with each other before you were born.

"And they still come to me, don't they?"

Yes, sometimes still, but rarely, they come to work with you.

"Why?"

They pop in to manipulate your system, to help you further align with spiritual energies that will serve you and your work.

"Like the time when Enoch and his crew showed up? That was pretty intense!"

Remember the feeling you had then, when you became conscious of the fact that you were with others in another place?

"I could never forget that!"

Then tell it.

"I wanted to celebrate big time because meeting the ones in charge of the whole operation felt like my reward for being such a willing participant for so many years. I felt overwhelmed because I knew I was having both my initiation and my graduation."

Your feelings were right because that was when your work with these particular beings was completed. And I tell you that all of it was but preparation so that you and I can now be having this exchange.

Throughout your life, you have met many other such beings who have worked on you while you have been sleeping. You have even had the fortunate opportunity to meet one, befriend him and have him work on you in the waking world. You have seen firsthand the phenomenal things that he is able to do, have you not?

"Yes, I have."

Then do you not have the validation you were looking for?

"I just had to hear it from You. Now will You tell me more about angels?"

Angels have the capacity to circumnavigate throughout the universe with no hardware crafts or ships, because, as I said, each one travels within its own merkabah. They are often visible in the night skies around the world and are mistaken for alien visitations. But the ones I describe here are not extra-terrestrials. They are more highly evolved sentient beings—celestials or ultra-terrestrials. In some parts of the world, they are dubbed masters and avatars. Elsewhere, they are called angelic, archangelic or super-angelic.

The purpose of these guides, angels and archangels (master thought- and light-forms) is to help everyone with their spiritual development. Yes, the Divine Hierarchy is always with you and has been present throughout Earth's history, co-creating all events up to now and the magnificent event that the world is leading up to.

"I don't mean to backtrack, but why do so many different types of aliens come?"

Backtrack all you like, Beloved, because you are right. Along with angels, highly evolved extra-terrestrial beings have been visiting your planet for a very long time. In fact, they have seeded Earth with much of its life and have had a hand in its unfoldment since the very beginning. You might say they are just watching over their investment.

"Wow, that's some interesting new data, but what do You mean by 'investment'?"

Information is your missing link, My Friend, and I have just given you a large chunk of it. Scientists have tried and will forever try to find the missing link in some fossil of a monkey-man, animal or plant frozen in the middle of its adaptation process. But the way things have actually evolved from one form into another is a little more complicated. I will not go into it now because then you would know everything about evolution, and that would negate the point of it entirely.

"So I'll ask something else. What about not-so-evolved aliens, why do they come?"

Because most of them are like moths to a flame and Earth is so divinely lit that they want to see what all the commotion is about. Did you know that Earth is becoming a star?

"I didn't think it could do that. How?"

I am saying that Earth is all the buzz and the universal gaze is upon you! Everything you do is viewed as a source for further learning by the many beings afloat in the cosmic life stream. And what they learn from you will enable their civilizations, which may be going through a similar period of elevation, to reach the next level.

"Are all who are watching us going to ascend when humanity does?"

Most of your visitors are readying to shift into the higher reality along with you. While, for others, this octave and higher ones are just too difficult to reach at this time.

"I know You've already told me a lot, but, if You don't mind, I still have a few more questions."

Sure, go ahead, I have all the time you need.

"What are their crafts made of?"

Many of their conveyances are made of minerals mined from their own planets as well as from other places in the universe.

"And do they actually appear in the sky or just in our minds?"

There are many such beings in your skies as well as in your consciousness spectrum.

"Why is it that they can't be seen by everyone?"

Most people are not open to seeing them because they are not ready to accept such phenomena. Nor are they ready to handle the fact that more are coming.

"Are we that special to these others?"

As I said, you are getting all this attention because you are considered to be universal royalty. In all the cosmos, no species except humans can attain God-realization, for only you contain the imprints, implants and genetic blueprints of the many complex forms it takes to do so. Those who have become a part of you have willingly volunteered to join in My experiment to unite humanity and Divinity into one upon the physical plane.

"Did the Heaven on Earth idea start with Adam and Eve?"

They were the seed for an Adamic people. But as I said earlier, there was interference from the fallen nephelim (fallen angels), and the distortions they caused needed to be corrected. It is for this reason that Adam and Eve's third son Seth was born. His purpose was to upgrade the human RNA/DNA code.

Lineage after lineage, these enhanced genetic codes have passed down from the House of David, until they have become woven into perfection for the arrival of Jesus. Can you see the Divine Order here?

"Unmistakably!"

Only because of such preparation was Jesus able to come as the Bearer of Christ Light. The life He lived then serves as the template you can follow now to unleash the dormant genetics within you that will help you reach your own divinity. Yes, through the lineage of Seth, Abraham, Moses, David and many others on a list too long to detail, Heaven on Earth is now possible. You see, God *is* patient.

"Extremely! And I'm sure many others would join me in

thanking You for that."

But you must also know that these spiritual ones that came to Earth did not come to solve *all* the world's problems. Indeed, because everything tainted has not yet been cleansed, each of you must do *your* part to eliminate the wickedness leftover by the fallen angels. If your predecessors had finished the job, Heaven on Earth would already be established. Look around. Is it?

"Far from it!"

So you see that there is more work yet to be done?

"Yes, I see."

That is why you and the others volunteered to come to Earth—to complete what the spiritual ones before you started, to help rectify the Luciferian energies of control and greed. And now that so many of you are becoming enlightened, others can follow your example and make the conscious choice to live in accordance with My plan.

"Please tell me more about our mission as light workers."

One purpose of your volunteer effort is to deal with your own karma as well as the karmic leftovers of anyone who has died. You see, no matter how you have lived, when you die, you may leave residue behind. But light workers have the ability and the duty to clean it up. I know you might think that you have been left holding the bag, but you must consider it an honor to see this mission through to completion.

"Please give me an example of this cleansing process."

The Bible recounts how Moses and the Israelites wandered through the desert for forty years because they were told not to cross over into the land of Jordan until their tribe had become purified; that only then could they begin anew. This same cleansing cycle occurred in Noah's time, in Sodom and Gomorrah, Atlantis, Lemuria (Mu), among others. Nothing has changed. This cleansing cycle always happens by collective choice, conscious or not.

"Can our mission fail?"

Yes.

"But will it?"

Not likely. You are here to succeed, Beloved, so be confident that you have what it takes to fulfill the work I am describing. Your task is not as tough as you may think. All you must do is be willing to make room for change within yourselves, and you do that by loving yourselves and expressing your love to those around you.

"I know I've grown to love myself more, but sometimes that's so hard to do, especially when I'm knee-deep in my issues."

But, Keith, you have pulled through most of your trials quite nicely, have you not? Now, as you work to deal with the others, you must make sure to keep plenty of Love on tap so that you can best handle whatever may be placed in front of you.

"That seems like such a tall order!"

Yes, it is. But you can do it. Many of you are doing it already.

"What do You mean by that?"

What I mean is that many of My tailors are already sewing away, helping to mend the rend in the universal tapestry torn asunder in the great fall. In your collective hands you hold all the tools, so please put to rest any concerns about your safety and the consequences of such vital and overdue change.

———◆———

As the world begins the new millennium, powerful forces of nature are becoming restless. But I suggest that, rather than be alarmed, you consider them a reveille, a wakeup call to alert you for what may come.

I do not bring this up to generate fear in you, Dear Ones. I do it to encourage you to take a closer look at what is transpiring.

Many of you can already feel the changes that are going on *within* yourselves, but you must look for the synchronicity *outside*, because your progress can best be gauged by viewing what is going on around you. The sooner humanity heals its collective emotional self, the sooner you will no longer face calamities like the ones that are beginning to beset you.

"I know lots of people who don't buy into this prophecy stuff because they've been told the world was going to end so many times and nothing's ever happened."

Yes, there are many whose hearts have closed and whose minds are now filled with skepticism. They feel they have been had and that those visionaries you mention have nothing better to do than perpetrate such hoaxes. But their lack of understanding only shows their lack of faith. It is almost as if they *want* the visions to come to pass so that they can believe there is some sort of true guidance on the planet to help them feel secure when something of great magnitude does transpire. But it does not matter if people believe or not, what does matter is that you and they must not accept any of it as a punishing god's wrath on a sinful world.

"Knowing that and knowing what I know, I still sometimes catch myself feeling scared when I think about some of the prophecies I've heard about actually coming to pass."

As I said earlier, prophecy is not restricted to what only the seers may have seen. Since *you* have the same capacity for vision as they, *you* can change the outcome of any prophecy simply by not seeing it in your future. Know that if a prophecy does not come true, it could very well be because its purpose has already been fulfilled. Still, everyone must keep their eyes wide open so that you can pick up on any potential visions that may be aligned and accurate.

Dear Ones, you do not need a seer to tell you how shaken your global snow globe is. That you can do for yourselves!

"Please tell me about some of the abuses that are going on and what Mother Earth is doing to defend herself against them."

Just like you, Keith, Mother Earth wants nothing more than to be healed. Those who continue to plunder her resources have not taken into consideration that they are violating a living, breathing being. They do not understand that they are making her gasp for air.

Her rainforests—her very lungs—are being depleted at such an alarming rate that, to catch her breath, she must exhale ever more powerful tornadoes and hurricanes.

Her oceans and rivers—the veins that oxygenate her heart—are being poisoned with so much industrial, nuclear and petro-chemical waste that much of the aquatic life that has long helped maintain her planetary balance is being destroyed. So, to cleanse her lifeblood, to give herself a transfusion so to speak, she must elevate her sea levels and make her rivers overflow.

In the frenzy to extract oil, her delicate flesh is being raided by thousands of daily drill punctures. The overuse of fossil fuel is depleting her ozone layer, giving rise to the fever of global warming. These violations make her belly rumble, shaking the ground beneath your feet.

Yet, despite all Mother Earth's signals, despite her valiant efforts, too many greedy ones refuse to care about her desperate plight. How much more of this torture do you think she can or will take?

"Probably not much."

That you can count on, Beloved.

Let Me ask you, Keith, what would you do if *you* were ill?

"I'd go see a doctor to be cured!"

Well, Mother Earth is following your advice, because she has come to Me, Dr. Love, for a prescription to cure her woes. She has been waiting for My okay to release the stresses caused by the greed and gluttony of the oblivious. Now that the time is right, I have given her the go sign and,

129

with extreme measures, she is moving forward.

But, even though her cataclysmic movement and climatic extremes do indeed point toward the prophesied "end times," the inevitable *can* be thwarted if everyone comes together.

"I'm thinking that might take an even more frightening event, like an asteroid heading towards us, something that threatens the existence of the entire human race."

You are so right. Something of that magnitude would surely cause everyone to put aside their racial, religious and territorial differences. If I were you, I would not wait long to do something about it.

"Are You saying that if we do somehow manage to pull together, these events might not happen?"

Yes, because then there would be no point. I told you before, I tell you now and I will tell you however many more times it takes, My Will is unity. So why not put your collective minds and hearts to their best use? Why not manifest together a peaceful and happy home on your planet? Know that no matter what you choose, what becomes of humanity is entirely up to you.

"Are we really that hard-headed? I mean, why would we be so foolish as to not do something to save our planet and ourselves? It makes me wonder what other civilizations in the universe think of our attitude."

Since you asked, I shall tell you.

Throughout the universe, humans are famous for being impervious to My Love and Will. From the toughness of your skin, to the hardness of your hearts; from hiding behind false ideas generated by fear, to your lack of perception brought about by ignorance, you are regarded as comfortably numb to the calamities you have created.

"I've got to agree with You. I think a lot of what's happening in the world is because we're so arrogant. And I think that we don't want to admit to ourselves that we really don't know as much about God as we think we do."

Good observation. And that brings Me to some important questions for everyone: Are you prepared to deal with the consequences of your ignorance? Are you ready to face the global catastrophes that can happen if the majority does nothing? Or are you ready and willing to get to know God and to learn and abide by the spiritual laws that, make no mistake about it, are very much in force?

People should not think that they must stop doing anything for themselves in order to do what they can to better the world. But they must understand that if they choose not to become involved with healing *both* themselves and the planet, the lives they are living will take a back seat to what will be happening around them.

Dear Ones, know that it is because I love you so much that I now relate the possibilities for dire events. And it is also out of Love that I say that it will benefit everyone so much more if you decide to see and make changes, rather than wait until the changes make you see. For only if you all begin to heal yourselves emotionally, can you triumphantly come together, so that all those dire predictions will have been for naught.

———•◆•———

These are the events that are potentially headed your way.

THE ECONOMY

The world's economy will collapse and your funds will have no worth. Yes, the very thing many have valued above all will become valueless.

The recent economic downturn in Japan must surely indicate to you that if such a crash can happen in that prosperous nation, no country is safe from such a fate.

But though the world's nations may falter economically, it does not mean that many people will not prosper individually. Those who have developed a prosperity consciousness will be able to manifest what is needed, not only for themselves, but for others close to them.

EXTRATERRESTRIALS

You are not alone! These beings are both present and benevolent, and they possess the knowledge to liberate you more quickly.

The more that extraterrestrials make their presence known, the more people will head for churches in droves, hoping to find some answers about why they are here. Yes, they may go once, but many will decide never to go back because no one there will be able to provide the answers they seek.

The earth will rumble.
The water will rise.
The weather will be extreme.
Volcanoes will come alive.

EARTHQUAKES

The earth will roll where you never thought it would. The whole planet will move to the beat of the universal drum!

WATER

Deluge and dearth — abundant where it normally is not; absent from where it once was.

TORNADOES

What you know as tornado alleys and tornado seasons will become things of the past. These mighty winds will occur randomly all year long and descend upon areas never hit before. If you follow the weather reports, you will notice such phenomena already occurring.

HURRICANES

There is great potential for colossal hurricanes. Many coastal areas face probable destruction. The damage wrought may seem beyond repair, but restoration will be accomplished. Tornadoes will accompany hurricanes on their eastward side.

133

VOLCANOES

These five hundred sleeping giants are already awakening and no continent will escape unscathed.

Those recent fires that have raged in Indonesia, Guatemala, Brazil, Mexico, Malaysia and elsewhere across the planet were ignited, not only by the droughts caused by global warming, but by the earth's magma rising to the surface.

Believe Me when I tell you, Dear Ones, that the Ring of Fire is alive!

WORLD LEADERS AND GOVERNMENTS

The true agenda of many governments and governmental figures worldwide will be brought to light.

The United States—"the greatest country of all" with "the greatest form of government"—will suffer a major breakdown. Its present legislative branch will collapse, and it will take years to rebuild it. Because of this restoration process, many old guard politicians will be forced out. Your new lawmakers will not make law, *per se*, but rather, will introduce you to Divine Law and teach you how to fall into flow with It. The establishment of Divine Order is commencing as I speak!

ILLNESS AND DISEASE

Many diseases once thought to be eradicated will again rear their ugly heads and baffling new viruses will spread. The record-breaking numbers of tuberculosis cases will increase. There could soon be more outbreaks of anthrax all over the world, with a very high potential in Jerusalem. More dread diseases will likely claim countless lives and leave many others disrupted in their wake.

STRANGE HAPPENINGS

What will you do when there are sightings of creatures never before known to man? What will you do when events that you never thought were possible begin to occur? Again I ask, *what will you do?*

————•————

I offer this itemized list of changes in form to let you know what the future may hold if everyone does not do what they can to lift global consciousness. And along with it, I emphatically remind you all that *every fearful subject you are reading about in this chapter can be avoided!*

I say to those who regard yourselves as human beings first and spiritual beings second: as long as you hold on to your ideas about what you think I am or should be—as long as you insist on denying your origin—you will not be able to thwart anything nor will you be able to cross the bridge from Earth to the Divine. For My Laws never conform to anyone's expectations nor will they ever change.

Once the world seeks God within,
sustained by God the world will be!

Some may continue to do nothing and insist that everything I have just attested to is bunk. My response to this is: how *can* it be? When this book circulates, the dormant power of many newly conscious people will come into play to help change upcoming events. What I am saying is that the chances for the world to make higher choices will increase.

"I know I should be okay with this by now, but can You tell me again why You have come to *me* with this information?"

I come *through* you, Beloved, because you are already keenly aware of all the potential changes and because you are open to My message.

"What if this prophetic stuff doesn't come true?"

Do you want it to?

"No, of course not! I was just wondering . . . "

Wonder no more. Did you ever stop to think that if any of these prophecies do not manifest, it could be because of people like you who are bringing forth what is required to cause them not to happen? That has been My goal all along—to give you what you need to know so that you can tell people about the great opportunity they now have to become My alchemists right along with you.

"Once again it seems as though You're concerned about the world and I'm worrying about me."

It is okay if you are worried about yourself, Keith. What I am asking you to do is a lot for anyone to take on.

"Thanks, I needed that."

But wait, there's more.

WEST COAST

Be on the lookout for the big one to hit early in the new millennium. Since you have chosen to live on or near a major fault line, you all know the risk. But you can modify what is likely coming your way by surrounding your entire region with light. Yes, with your collective power, you can forestall this dreadful event.

EAST COAST

Early in the new millennium, colossal hurricanes will pound your coastal areas, causing mudslides and floods. Many, fearing a tidal wave, will have already moved inland. Your good news is that you have the same collective power that those on the West Coast have and you can alter these awful events as well.

MIDDLE AMERICA

There is great potential that your entire landmass will undergo dramatic shifts. The Mississippi River will grow to many times its present size, creating a large division between east and west. Great bridges will have to be built so that you can travel from one side to the other.

PEOPLE OF THE WORLD

No matter where you reside, it is crucial that you watch for the signs. If there is not enough spiritual light being generated where you live, move. Look to the Hopi Indian map for places that are safe and stable. A more current reference is the *I Am America Map*. These two put forth an amazingly accurate outline of the New Land of the Dove, the New Place of Peace.

How can you possibly think that God does not speak to anyone but the chosen few? How can you possibly think there are "a chosen few"? The fact of the matter is, I speak to everyone—but only the chosen few choose to listen.

"Am I right in saying that water's in almost everything You just listed?"

It is no accident that water plays such a large and powerful part in the planetary cleansing process, for water is the physical manifestation of emotions and the subconscious. Keith, have you not noticed how turbulent water dreams have helped to reveal and resolve some of your own internal conflicts?

"Yes, but all this stuff You're saying is really scary."

I am aware that these planetary changes I speak of are causing and will cause much fear. But, as I have said before, My intention is not to alarm. My intention is to help you realize that the more you align yourselves with the message of this book (and the others you may come across that are filled with truth), the better you will be prepared for whatever comes.

"Okay. I understand all this stuff *can* happen. But why does it *have* to?"

The only thing that *has* to happen before such events can be prevented is that everyone's present emotional and spiritual energies must transform. The good thing is that even though most of you have waited until now to take up

My Cause in earnest, coming together of your own freewill can and will dramatically alter your fate.

The sad thing is that most of humanity has not yet chosen to live the very life that it will be living after these changes do occur.

Just visualize it, Beloved—everyone pitching in, everyone helping each other so that the entire human experience can be elevated. You can call it *Anchoring Heaven On Earth*. Should be a book, huh?

"Sounds like a great title to me!" (grinning a knowing grin)

We have covered quite a lot of ground here, have we not?

"Yes we have, and I think I've gotten a handle on the bigger picture at least."

Good, My Friend. Now, before we call it a day, I offer this gentle message for all:

I have prepared a place for your Homecoming where you will be lovingly received into My Light. Yes, the door to the universe will open for you if you take this opportunity to understand change and to change—to learn how to stand strong in this time of change.

And, lastly, some wise words from My friend,
John Lennon:

"ALL YOU NEED IS LOVE"

*The highest ideal
is to have such
an awareness shift
that God's Love
is the only thing
you see, think, feel
and therefore, are!*

Opening Up and Grounding
The Divine Principle

I now offer some specific suggestions to help you achieve the peace that will allow you to become your Higher Self. As this information comes to you, do what you have learned—just let go and relax. Soon such a state will be a constant in your life.

———— •♦• ————

The two techniques I present here are called Opening and Grounding. Intentionally making them a part of your daily practice will make you much more available to Divine energy. Although these disciplines are not new to you, Keith, they probably are to most with whom you will share this work. But I assure you that with My help and everyone's desire to come to peace, success for all of you is guaranteed. Let us begin.

I shall now tell you about your body's vital energy centers, the chakras. Each of you has seven chakras ascending from the base of your spine to the top of your head. Each chakra is associated with an aspect of consciousness and each one is an interface for the flow of your life energy. Although chakras are not measurable scientifically, believe Me, they do exist and you must learn to intentionally balance them to live a productive, healthy life.

"Are we going to work with all of them?"

No, just three, for they will enhance all the others.

OPENING YOUR CHAKRAS THROUGH VISUALIZATION

You might find it helpful at first to record this guided meditation until you become more familiar with how to do it. Here we go.

Create a special place for yourself somewhere in your home. Soft music, candles and incense can help, but they are not essential. Once you get comfortable in a sitting or prone position, begin to breathe in and out evenly and continually, gradually bringing your in-breath and out-breath into one smooth circular sequence. Look to connect your in-breath with God and your out-breath with releasing the negativity you have accumulated your whole life long.

After you feel you have achieved a state of stillness, place your left hand over the center of your chest—on the heart chakra, your love center. See its color as green.

As you continue to breathe in and out, in and out, imagine a great burst of green light in this area—an ever-expanding ray that starts in the heart and moves beyond the parameters of your body. Imagine that this light then moves out from you and begins to encompass your home, neighborhood, city, state, country, continent and the Earth. Once you have embraced this image, hold it for a few moments, thank God, and notice your newfound calm. Then, when you feel you are ready, bring your attention back to the room and press the STOP button on your recorder.

Using this technique will make it much easier for you to begin to accept trust and love, for it is your resistance to these two that has caused you to close off your emotional self in the first place.

"What difference does it make which hand I use?"

Using your left hand is a function of the right side of your brain, the home of your intuitive side. So when you place your left hand over your heart, you are saying to Spirit, "Through my heart that guides me, I accept the information and energy that benefits me." Saying this out loud adds even more power to the exercise.

Let Me paint a scenario that will help you to see how this technique works:

You are in an unfamiliar room. The light is off. You tread carefully because you do not wish to bump into any furniture. Even in the darkness, your intent to see is evident as you fumble around for the light switch. Spirit embraces this intent and guides your hand to that elusive switch—your "in-light-in-meant."

Once you flick it, what has eluded you for far too long will be illuminated and you will be able to clearly see your spiritual path. This is the light you must be drawn to,

143

Beloved, to encounter all that will best serve you.

Using such light visualizations will benefit you beyond what you can grasp right now. Their profound power begins at the quantum thought level and moves to the sub-atomic level. From the subatomic level, it progresses to the atomic level. Next, it goes to the molecular level and, lastly, to the cellular level. All these levels require new imprints and codes before light activity can become constant. So the more you practice, the better your results will be.

Do you remember last night when the three Light Beings came to you while you slept?

"Yes I do."

They came to tune you up a bit, Keith, to help you acclimate to the new vibrations in your energy matrix. Now you are even more ready to entertain light-thoughts and use them for those who are in need of healing energies, for events that need uplifting and for other purposes that will bring about expansion. But do not forget to do it for yourself—to always fill and surround yourself with light. I remind you that each of you has a signature vibration, a frequency unlike any other person's, that attracts your previous actions to you. So the more light you embody and emanate, the more negative energy you will be able to keep at bay.

———◆·———

I shall now speak of Grounding.

Grounding takes place when you pull your True Self

(your Soul) down from the higher plane to live on Earth (in your body). Why should you do this? Because, like electricity, you, too, must be grounded in order to function, in order to maintain stability in both your body and your life.

The energy center that needs to be balanced for grounding the Soul is your root chakra. This chakra is located just below the base of the spine and its color is red. One who lives in Love has a root chakra that is always open.

"Are You trying to tell me that something I'm doing or not doing is causing my problems?"

Yes and no, Keith. Sometimes you *do* do something that throws your root chakra out of balance. Sometimes suppressed issues come up and that is what throws it out. This does not mean that you are consistently doing something incorrectly, but balancing your root chakra *will* provide a buffer for some of those headaches of yours.

You see, in this period of high-energy movement, Spirit is beginning to reverberate in the temple of your heart and a Love deeper than any you have ever known is beginning to emerge. But, in order for It to do so, everything else (your grief, anger, fear, etc.) must be pushed outward into the physical world so you can view it and clear it away. This explains why things sometimes get shaky even when they seem to be going so well.

"So, despite my doubts, everything's okay?"

Yes, everything is just fine. It may help if you compare this grounding process to the stroking of a pure crystal wineglass. When the glass's rim is rubbed, its resonating properties are activated. Likewise, *you* are beginning to resonate, because you are being touched by frequencies of the Holy Spirit.

"I understand what You've just said, but how am I supposed to stay motivated to ground myself if doing so only invites more trouble?"

Grounding is not the cause of your troubles but it *will* be the end of them because grounding your Self will help you deal with the movement of such energies and eventually clear them.

Up until relatively recently, you did not even realize that you had a root chakra and you did not know that if your root chakra is unbalanced, the other centers in the body cannot possibly function properly. You did not know that neglect of this center invites problems such as fatigue, depression, deteriorating health and eventually, an untimely, premature death.

Now that you do know these indispensable facts, you realize how important it is to show your intent for grounding as often as you can. Not to worry, Beloved. More bearers of My Light will appear to help you with this chakra—to help you get out and stay out of that wobbly state yourself.

"And just in time, huh?"

Well, let us just say that by showing your intent to be balanced and in touch with your Divine nature, you are showing intent to remain upon the earth plane.

"Oh Lordy, I'm not ready to go just yet! What do You suggest I do?"

Keep praying and meditating, and continuing to make

the effort to be of service to all. In other words, just keep doing what you are doing and you will be fine.

GROUNDING YOURSELF THROUGH VISUALIZATION

I suggest once again that until you become familiar with this process, a taping device may be helpful. That way you can let your own voice guide your meditation.

Go once again to the place you have created for yourself. When you are settled and comfortable, begin the circular breathing you have learned—in and out, in and out, in and out. Breathe in God and exhale fear. Let go of mundane thoughts and all worldly issues that consume your mind.

Now, just imagine a white light entering through the top of your head. This point of entry is the crown chakra, the vortex to God's Will and Knowing. See its color as violet. As the white light courses its way to your heart, observe it as it segues into a soft shade of pink. Hold this image for a while as you continue your circular breathing. Exhale any worries you may have and breathe in God.

Bring this pink light down towards your coccyx (tailbone). See the light turn into a rich shade of red and, as you rhythmically breathe, allow it to do its magic and bring stability to this area.

Next, visualize the vivid red light that has been centered in your coccyx flowing out from you, penetrating the earth and rooting itself into the ground. See the image of a tree taking root, if you like. Then visualize the light in all the chakras you have been meditating on all at once and take this moment to see yourself as balanced. Then, thank God once more for guiding you to your newfound stability. You are now grounded.

Do this meditation daily, preferably in the morning. You can actually perform it at any time throughout the day, even while you are taking a walk, because doing anything that touches your feet to Mother Earth is another good way for you to show your intent to better deal with the shaky things in your life.

Keith, can you tell me how many times you have shut your emotions down for whatever reason, only to have your entire system go into clampdown mode, too?

"I've got a pretty good idea, but I'm sure You can enlighten me some more."

I certainly can. Did you know that you got that kidney stone because you kept your emotions so locked up? Shall we talk about that for a bit?

"This won't hurt, will it?"

Not as much as the kidney stone.

"That's a relief."

What happened was that your emotional energy became hard as stone because your system was so heavily blocked. That is why you woke up one morning to find yourself stuck *with* and stuck *by* that excruciating pellet. Your stubbornness manifested in a most profound and undeniable way, did it not?

"It hurts just to talk about it!"

Ah, but we must!

Your kidney stone crisis can be likened to what happens

when water (urine) tries to course its way through a dirt-clogged (stone-clogged) pipe (urinary tract). Eventually fresh water flows, but not until the pipes have gone through a thorough cleaning.

Now that you have realized that you are the pipe, you know you must continue to use the grounding meditation so that the perpetual current of the Divine Spigot can move emotional energy through you without inhibition.

"I pray I have completely learned that lesson!"

I know you have been through hurtful times, Beloved, and have sworn on your Soul that you would never again become so vulnerable. Must I remind you that it is this very resistance that has stopped trust and love from becoming anchored within you?

Keith, you must pay close attention to every signal your body sends you and take action every time you suspect a potential blockage. If you continue to ignore them, one day you will find your emotional reservoir drained, leaving you with nothing but sludge.

I can hear you thinking, "Oh no, must I go through this again?" And I say "Yes, but this time, you will be well-prepared, better able to realize that it is just as easy to keep your emotional pipes cleared out as it was to get them all clogged up to begin with. Lest you forget, you have Me as your Plumber, and I come equipped with a very special auger.

"That's so comforting for me to hear. Is there anything else I should be doing to help myself?"

Glad you asked, because here is a third technique that will allow you to even further open and ground your Self.

It is a mantra to be repeated in meditation until you intuitively feel that you are balanced.

I lovingly command
all the chakras in my energy matrix
to open and maintain a state of perfect balance —
to open and tune in to the vibration of Om.

Earlier, I mentioned some rules and laws to you. I shall now elaborate.

What currently serves as the planet's laws are not, for they are false. I ask you: How can you break a law — how?

"I don't understand Your question."

Since a law is stable and absolute, it cannot be broken. That is what makes it law. If laws could be broken, the universe would shut down. Spiritual law is what maintains universal order and what makes My existence eternal.

So many of you are still flouting universal law by following false rulers, thus their false rules — and you have been bending them at that. Can you see how this relates to the trouble you are having?

"I'm starting to. Will You show me what spiritual law looks like?"

I will do you one better by giving you the Divine Principle, My Law, everything that I am. When you live It — when you let It become anchored within you — Heaven on Earth will be yours.

The Divine Principle

1) Choose not to accept defeat.

The Law of All Possibilities,
Pure Potentiality and Godhood

*Having absolute faith in your Self
will enable you to see that
miracles can happen to you.
That is when you will truly begin
to live your life as a God aspirant.*

2) Show no intent to control, for any such attempt will defeat you.

The Law of Karma/The Law of Cause and Effect

Through this Law, Divine Order is upheld.

3) Choose not to place your happiness in the hands of another person, nor in the temporal world.

The Law of Self-fulfillment through God,
the Source of all life and happiness

*The law of no external idol worship
was given to you by Moses.*

4) Choose to reach for the Ideal Self by turning inward to move forward.

The Law of Observation

Learning to remember creates regeneration, expansion and conscious spiritual evolution.

5) Pray and meditate daily.

The Law of Giving and Receiving

Prayer is talking to God; meditation is listening. When these two are practiced together, you and I communicate.

Prayer is Giving. When you pray, you help heal someone or give them something they may be in need of.

Giving is Receiving. When you give, you affirm that you have an abundance to share and the gift becomes your own.

Meditation is Receiving. When you meditate, the Soul's wisdom is revealed to you and the potential for betterment becomes clear.

Receiving is Giving. When you receive something gratefully, it allows another to feel the joy of giving. Thus is abundance spread.

6) Show intent to embrace, understand and transcend your fear.

The Law of Divinity and Freewill Choice

Aligning with God
rewards you with everlasting peace.

7) Become fully aware of what you are thinking and feeling, for this will launch you into your mastery as Creator.

The Law of "I"

When you are aware of awareness,
you are conscious of consciousness.

8) Take responsibility for your life, for it is your own creation — all of it!

The Law of Deliberate Creativity

Living Laws 1 and 7.

9) Claim your part in the Whole by realizing who you are. You are God — I am you!

The Law of Self-Enlightenment

Acknowledging God as Omniscient,
Omnipresent, Omnipotent —
the Divine Source Principle
embodied within all things.

Inherent in each of these Laws is the whole of the Divine Principle. It will take your heart to fully comprehend them because they are formless, above and beyond language. But the sooner you begin to open yourself to them, ground them and master them, the sooner you can come Home. There is no need to wait until death for life, for living by My Divine Principles will grant you life throughout your life.

———— • ————

As you continue working, you might come up against more Self-testing hurdles. Do not be overly concerned, because jumping them is what has to happen before the Divine Principle can become anchored within you.

"You mean, for instance, when someone tells me, 'What you are doing may be the work of the devil'?"

It makes you think, does it not?

"Yes, it sure does."

Little do you both know that when people say such things they are giving you a gift! Yes, by simply observing their attitudes about you and your work, you get another chance to see how far you have come.

I enjoy watching you, Keith, as you effort to stay centered when you interact with those who confront you about the themes we touch on in this book. Do you not feel a sense of accomplishment every time you recognize someone's fear-based posture as a mirror of your own ego's attempt to sustain its reign as king of your spiritual hill?

"Yes I do, but sometimes I get so caught up in the dynamic."

Whenever you feel that happening, try implementing the opening technique I just taught you, for it will launch you deeper into Spirit and help you not to react to anyone who tries to give you hell.

"You sure use that word 'hell' a lot. Why?"

To help you to see that you are the ones who create it. Some examples: A person who believes that I do not provide believes that they have nothing to give. A person who believes in a judgmental god believes they must judge others. A person who believes in a punishing god believes they must punish others, and so on. The way you think I treat you is the way you treat the world around you. My point is, for those who do not choose to know Me as I truly am, hell is a reality.

"I get it — it's all about what we believe!"

You are close. It is all about what you know. And if you truly know Me, Heaven is the only true reality. Regardless of your point of view, know that you will only "have rapport" with the God/god you see, think and feel.

Your life is your own creation!

Look into the mirror every day and ask yourself: "Do I like what I see and am I living my best life?" Try it—an answer will come through. And when it does, Who do you think will be providing it?

"Me — You?"

What is the difference?

"Wow! At the exact moment You were asking me that question, both my home phone and my cell phone rang."

That was just Me, Beloved, chiming in to remind you that there is no difference between us—that no matter how many of your mental phone lines may be ringing, there is only One Caller.

Yes, it was just Me reminding you to stay acutely aware because you still harbor a belief in separation. I know you will do your best to rid yourself of it. And I encourage not only you, but everyone, to live the Divine Principle so that you can discover what is real about yourselves, thus making all of you conscious co-creators.

Loved Ones, My Children,
open your eyes and expand your hearts!
Open yourselves to a Divine life
and I will rise up through you
as you all celebrate your expressions of Me.

Blessed be the ones who awaken.
Blessings, as well, to those who do not.

*Through the manner
in which you live
and by the standards you set,
people will have
the opportunity to see
what a higher life looks like.*

Your Gift of
Power and Freedom

As each of you becomes more aware of your own divinity, you will begin to see that global change begins with you alone — that you can affect the way things happen. Through the manner in which you live and by the standards you set, people will have the opportunity to see what a higher life looks like.

———— ◆ ————

Christ Jesus was a prime example of supreme living during His time upon Earth. By living a life of righteousness and peace, He was able to make a powerful impact and a profound difference. Some two thousand years later, His life is still the standard. He is still the Truth, the Hope, the Light and the Way. His teachings have inspired countless millions to live a pure and love-filled life, thus creating the energy needed for the whole world to shift.

Jesus searched for Me His entire early life, walking the land believing He was only a messenger. But as an adult, when he visited the Himalayan monasteries, He learned from the Masters who lived there to seek God within Himself, and He came to the realization that the external world was only a kaleidoscopic picture interpreted by His own mind. His pilgrimage was a great success in that it helped Him to realize that He was no longer just a messenger of God, but was now the Son of God. "I am in My Father, ye in Me and I in you." (John 14:20)

When Jesus stood upon the hill and spoke to the multitude, the young Teacher offered great wisdom, but few believed His words. In fact, many shouted, "Are You the Messiah? If You are truly the Messiah, then perform a miracle for us!" Because of their doubt and fear, people did not realize that the miracle was already there *in the form* of Jesus! He was there to *inform* them about their own freedom, their Divine nature and the fact that, indeed, they were no different from Him.

Can you see how so many missed their window of opportunity to reach spiritual liberation because they doubted that He was the Christ?

"Yes, I sure can. Why didn't they listen?"

Because Jesus appeared to be an ordinary man like everyone else. But soon enough, no one could deny His extraordinary Presence.

"Once people believed that He was who He said He was, why didn't they follow Him then?"

Because soldiers (using brute force if necessary) were regularly deployed to bring to a halt all the rabble-rousing that seemed to happen wherever He went. But despite all adversity, Jesus pushed on until the very end.

When that day came, Jesus accepted His death freely, thus showing those around Him how such an event is not the end of life, but only a transition to another level of being—the infinite and immortal change of the Atma, the Spirit. "For dust thou art, and unto dust shalt thou return." (Genesis 3:19)

In the centuries since Jesus' ascension, most have focused on His death instead of His life and His afterlife. People still seek Him on the cross but He is no longer there; as long as people continue to be bound to that image, they cannot begin to understand the crucifixion metaphor.

If you want to be a true follower of Christ, you must take Jesus down from that old rugged cross and move on with your life. Do you not understand that the Lamb was sacrificed then for your liberation now?

Let Me ask you a question. Does the fact that most in His time doubted that He was the Christed One detract from the truth about the One called Jesus?

"Not at all!"

I would expect that answer from you, Keith, because you are among those who already accept this 2000-year-old truth. But know that the cycle of doubt versus truth is happening yet again. Yes, there are many who have inherited the heirloom of doubt from those who questioned

Jesus on the hill. Their misgivings echo now as they did then. "If you 'New-agers' think you are Messiahs with your 'I am God' view, then perform a miracle for us!" they say.

I ask each of you: Do you want to be as those in Jesus' time, regarded by future generations as one of history's doubters? Your answers matter not, for no amount of doubt can take away the validity of the Messiah-ship appearing now to enlighten you about your freedom, power and oneness with God.

Freewill
The human will regarded as free from restraints, compulsions or any antecedent conditions; freedom of decision or choice.

Earth is Spirit's neutral zone, Beloved, and as one of its denizens, you have freewill on a freewill planet, able to opt for either Love or fear with every choice you make.

"But how do I recognize the highest choice so I can make it consistently?"

You are wise to recognize that that is exactly where you have been stuck. Even so, you have continued making choices. Some have manifested to your liking, while others have not.

We both know that Love is the choice you truly desire, but you must commit yourself more fully to It. You do that by doing even more intensive and extensive mind-cleansing and more conscious, intentful Soul-searching. That is what will get you there.

Back to basics. For clarity about how you ended up where you are now, it is time to check your origins and the many influences you have had along the way.

To learn about yourself on the physical level, you must go all the way back to your birth, birthplace and early environment. Recall your food intake, injuries that you sustained and illnesses that you had throughout your childhood.

To learn about yourself on a mental level, look to your family, religious instructors, peers, teachers, government and the media, for they instilled in you what they thought was right or wrong, holy or blasphemous, real or illusion, possible or impossible.

To learn about yourself on an emotional level, consider the hurt, pain and fear you have been through. Ask yourself: Why did I choose to incarnate into that particular family, in that particular place? What lessons did I come here to complete? Acknowledge how the tough love your parents meted out was not intended to abuse you nor was it meant to leave you holding any emotional baggage. Instead, take into account how their discipline has been instrumental to your development. Take stock of what you are holding onto and rejoice in what you have released. Take an overview of your life—the gift of it and the real gift of what you have gained by living it. See all these lessons and learn!

To get to your spiritual roots, understand that your body is comprised of the same properties as the celestial bodies, your star parents. Begin to see yourself as a Divine Child, enfolded by Universal Consciousness, coming into your purpose, your birthright and divinity. Look in, out and all about. *See God, be God!*

"Will it help for me to think of us humans as characters who have come to act out our roles on Earth's great stage of duality?"

Yes, because that is exactly what you are doing. Even though you do not remember this, long before everyone began to incarnate, you collectively decided how long you were willing to play your parts in the Earth experiment. You agreed that when the clock ran out, whatever level of consciousness you had achieved would be the determining factor for the world's fate.

"Why don't we remember?"

That is the only way that all your choices can be unbiased ones.

"I wish I could've known about who I am sooner."

Why?

"Maybe I could've done more while I've been here this time!"

It does not matter whether or not you knew — your next level will happen regardless. What is important is that you have the time of your life while you are here.

"I'm having a bunch of fun all right, but what I want is more quality."

Questions, Keith.

"Huh?"

Use that exquisite and ever-present inquisitiveness of yours to ask questions like: Who am I? Why am I here?

Why do things happen to me the way they do? What does it all mean? No matter the question, if you ask it with all your heart, the door to the answer will swing open, revealing the "I" that you truly are, and then your life will be one of superior quality.

The "I" within you is subtler than you yet realize, and sometimes you try so hard to experience it that you overshoot your target. What you are looking for lies in wait just behind the mask of what you know as you. To merge with it, just relax into it. You will know you are there when you recognize how very much you have let yourself become a slave to your own thoughts and feelings.

Try this. Turn some music on that moves you and get lost in it like you love to do.

"Okay."

Are you listening with just your ears?

"No, no, *all* of me is listening and I'm amazed how quickly I was able to tune in to the True Listener."

Well, that sweet spot of your Soul is the eternal, unchanging, ever aware "I," and it has always been there, just waiting.

"My whole life I've looked for it so hard and this whole time it's been right under my nose. No wonder I've been so frustrated!"

I know that it sometimes gets quite hectic for you, but even your irritation is purposeful on the spiritual road to perfection.

"I just wish I could experience who I really am on a daily basis."

165

Yes, you frequently change your "I" perspective, claiming you are this or that now, trying to be something, anything—all the while harboring great hopes of discovering who you *really* are. You have no trouble saying "I, I, I," but you have so much trouble experiencing your own authenticity.

What will help is when you begin to change your internal dialogue about who and what you think you are. It does not help you one iota to say things like: "I am angry. I am mad. I am sick. I am content. I am bored. I am alone. I am poor. I am afraid."

"You are so right!"

Yes, you are.

"Me?"

There, you did it again.

"Did what?"

So easily overlooked your True Self. And that, My Friend, is what causes your difficulty. Understand that you are not the feelings that flood your emotional system nor are you the thoughts that overwhelm your mind. As you have just realized, *you* are the Silent Witness, observing the whole drama as it unfolds. But the problem is that your ego is not so silent! It wants to be the director and continue to dictate to you exactly what it thinks you are, should be and should do. The confusion it engenders often pulls you into life's dramatic movie even further, convincing you that whatever you are experiencing is real.

No wonder the life you are living seems to be the same thing over and over again. You see, Beloved, when you make judgments based solely upon past experiences, you leave no room for something new. There are many times I hear you say to yourself, "What about me? When is it my turn?" Well, this book, this body, this life are *all* for you—the *real* you. Now go live your purpose! Now it *is* your turn.

———— ◆ • ————

Shall we play with some more words to facilitate a lesson?

"Sure."

If you look at the cliché of "me, myself and I," you might recognize the *"me"* in this saying as what you once thought yourself to be—separate, alone and detached. With this viewpoint, seeking self-gain was automatic for you. You did not have much choice in the matter because such an attitude is never about the true you; it is always about the ego and what it wants.

You must be willing to toss that "me" of yours into Love's purifying fires to ignite the flame of who you really are. You must not continue to let your ego steal from the Self that you are in order to appease the mirage self. You must turn your selfishness into selflessness.

"Any suggestions about how I can become more giving and allowing?"

You must reverse the formula from "me, myself and I" to "I, my Self and me." First see God ("I") as the totality of all things; next, honor the "Higher Self" in everyone; then accept everyone as they really are—facets of you ("me").

"Will living like this get me the Love I need so I can be more giving?"

Not quite. Your ego is still dictating to you that you have a lack of Love and that It must somehow be gained. But Love is not something you *get*—Love is something you *are*. It is the very stuff that you are made of—Me, My Self and I—God.

"Any other suggestions about how I can merge into the Self?"

Yes. Trust Me with your life. Surrendering the whole thing up to Me will ease you into Divine Order quite nicely.

"But that's so tough for me to do all the time."

I have never said that pursuing a Divine life would be easy, Keith, but My Reality is there for those who really want It.

"How do You do that?"

Do what?

"Cause me to feel so present with such simple words."

I have had a lot of practice and that is what I encourage you to do—practice, practice, practice!

I know how challenging living in your world can be, especially when its temptations keep you wanting much of what it has to offer. But you can free yourself from your bondage anytime you choose by making divinity your only want.

Lifetime after lifetime, you have tried so hard to be with Me. This time, stop trying! Just *be* with Me. Step back from your life's movie and see with your Divine Eye—the All

Knowing, All Seeing, Ever Present Eye, the Eye ("I") of God.

"So reincarnation awakens the Divine within us all so that one day we can anchor It on the earth plane?"

Yes, Beloved, all this time, you have been playing God's game of life and you did not even realize it.

"But why can't we know from the start that it's just a game?"

Because if you knew you would always be the winner, you would never play the game. And the game, after all, is the sole/Soul reason for your life. So just play for the sake of playing. Only when you do that can you advance to the next level.

Freedom

Freedom from slavery, captivity, or any other form of arbitrary control.

Departure from rules or procedures. Freedom.

As you continue aligning yourself with God, you will need some tools to remove any ego-weeds that may still be trying to stifle the growth of your Spirit's fruit. Till that fertile ground thoroughly so that it can germinate the seeds of Love and grow God in you.

"What can I use as my Miracle-Gro?"

Right now, prayer, for it will fertilize the Soul experiences that you so long to have. It will help you to be ever more conscious and to stay in the flow, allowing such things to happen more frequently.

Remember that one night a few years ago when I visited you in your blue-sky-dream?

"Yes..."

I came to you because I heard you pray for your spirit's freedom. Do you remember what I asked you?

"You asked me, 'What is it that you really, truly desire, Keith?'"

You did not know how to reply to My question, so I responded for you. "What you long to do is fly!" I said. You happily agreed and off we went. Did you enjoy your flight?

"Yeah, it was really neat! Did You?"

Dear One, I cannot begin to tell you what a delight it was then (and still is) for Me to observe your joyful free spirit when you take flight.

"How often do I fly?"

Nightly.

"Really?"

Yes.

"But I'm..."

...not always able to recall doing it. Yes, I know. Nothing would please Me more than if you were to become conscious of all your "out of body" excursions. Like I told you, you have but to pray to watch your miracles grow.

What you are efforting to accomplish nightly, shamanic cultures have already perfected. They have mastered the art of dream-walking and shape-shifting, and have learned how to take on the many forms of Spirit. Much of their time is spent asking Mother Earth for permission to see through the eyes of her animals and elementals and thus to experience various bandwidths unknown to most.

"Some believe that these tales of different realities are just hallucinations shamans have had as a result of smoking marijuana or taking peyote."

Even though ingesting these plant forms induces some of their visions, it does not mean that what they may see during them is not real. Such realities *do* exist; they have to, or shamans could not have the experiences they do.

"Are You suggesting that I go out and get some marijuana or peyote to take?"

No. But know that shamans use these substances for the right reasons when they feel it is necessary — to encourage spiritual expansion. They never do it just to "get high" or to escape from the reality of a bad life. They take great care to use these things responsibly, as stepping-stones to a "higher reality" and for the greater good.

"Why do I only have these way out experiences when I'm sleeping and not when I'm awake?"

Because, during sleep, you lose the very awareness of your body that you need to stay in it and because, as long as you are sleeping, you cannot be lured into the temptations of the external world that your mind and body crave.

"Sometimes I have dreams that seem so real that I wake up thinking I was actually there."

You were.

"I was?"

If you were not there, where were you?

"But aren't dreams just metaphors for something else?"

And your life on Earth is not?

"I see Your point."

You are dreaming right now, Dear One. You may think just because your physical eyes are open that you are awake. But even when they are open, there is a part of you that still sleeps.

"This dream vs. reality thing is still confusing me."

I shall effort to clear it up then. When you have a dream, it is a dream and, at the same time, it is not. In your waking state of consciousness, when everything seems to be tangible, that too is a dream. The reality is that both provide you with experiences that are integral to your growth. The dichotomy is that, since both are dreams dreamed from *My* Mind, everything in your waking and sleeping life is an illusion as well as real.

"I understand that. But if I'm faced with two scenarios, how can I decide which one is the higher and which one is the lower?"

Your ability to differentiate between the two is what makes one more real than the other. The one that you decide is a closer representation of Me is the higher reality. The other is more likely to be the illusion or the lower reality. But keep in mind this is only relative, because the decision between higher and lower can vary from person to person. And even though you deem something to be either real or illusory, do not lose sight of the real Truth — *that God is the Dreamer behind both.* Remember this and the you that sleeps with your eyes open will awaken to truly see My Reality.

"Does everyone dream when they sleep?"

Yes.

"But why doesn't everyone remember their dreams?"

Because many do not like what they see when they dream, so they subconsciously shut themselves off from remembering them.

"What's the difference between an out of body journey and a dream?"

You must understand that there is no such thing as out of body.

"But what about in death?"

The Soul does not leave the body; the body leaves the Soul. Or, said another way, the body is no longer animated, at least in the time frame of that person's life. However, the reality of that person's past remains active in the universe and so does his or her body. So no one ever really dies.

What happens in an out of body experience or in death is that one's consciousness shifts to another dimension of Spirit. That is what creates the sensation of movement or flying. In either case, you really do not go anywhere except deeper within, because the Soul is everywhere and everything.

The difference between an out of body experience and a dream is that one is an experience of another aspect of the Soul and the other is an experience of the mind and its many ideas.

"Does everyone have out of body jaunts nightly?"

You all go somewhere else to learn more about yourselves and the universe. But not everyone remembers these trips.

"Why not? Is it for the same reason that people don't remember their dreams — because what happened while they were 'out there' wasn't pleasant?"

No, not always.

"I don't understand. If they had a good experience, why wouldn't they want to remember it?"

Good question. A person has to pass through their mind before they can get back to their body. That is where things get a bit twisted and that is why they dream scary dreams.

"I see. There is mental confusion."

Yes, but it is for good cause. When someone's consciousness returns to the body, the mind must paint pictures to try to explain what they have just experienced on their journey. This is not an easy task when nothing in their mind represents anything they may have experienced while they were out. To many, that is downright frightening.

"I can see so much of myself in that explanation."

That is good, Keith. Take it all in and do the work that is required to free yourself from your fears so that you may be truly awake.

"What does it mean to be truly awake?"

You are spiritually awake when you no longer need to fall asleep to experience the Soul. And once you are illuminated, you will not experience a loss of awareness during the time your body needs to rest.

"Is there a difference between enlightenment and being

awake?"

Enlightenment is the process of awakening. Awake is the constant awareness that happens as a result of any true understanding. Once you realize something, it can never be un-realized, for it is impossible to do away with what you know — your ongoing expansion just keeps on going.

"What will happen after I awaken?"

You will find yourself in another reality (another dream) that will continue until you graduate to Dreamer status — God-realization.

"You mean there is more to do after I awaken?"

As I said before, My Reality is for those who really want it! Yes, the road is a long one and it will take time. But that road will eventually lead you to eternity and when you get there, all your struggles will be forgotten.

———— • ————

Loved One, I do not wish you to fall behind. Are you keeping up?

"Yes. Yes, I am . . . I think."

Good. Now for something very exciting. I say it this way because I know how much you like it when you have those far out experiences.

"I'm so ready!"

In the near future, you will be able to project your consciousness through portals that are opening all over the planet. These stargates will operate just like WINDOWS does on your computer, in that energy and distinctly different types of information will be displayed, but without all the hardware. The networking capabilities of *My* gateways will be the same as your Internet world, but they will let you have the universe at your fingertips.

"Really?"

Really. And you will need to take the same approach to have any success of passing through. First, you will have to boot yourself up through meditation. Second, you will have to sign on by submitting the correct password—responsibility. Third, you will have to wait to be processed before the Innernet Soul Provider—Me—will let you in.

Once you are logged on, you will then click on the Universal Library icon in your mind's eye, which will lead you to any cosmic experience or information you may be looking for. After doing your search and finding exactly what you are seeking, you will then be ready to surf the Information Super-natural Highway.

"Tell me more!" (laughing)

The software of the universal mainframe is formatted so that you can visit and browse on any cosmic web page for as long as you like. Then, when you are done, just sign off and begin to put the knowledge you gained from your surfing journey to use. Whatever you download will help you to execute your upgrading.

"Is it correct say that the computer and information age that we're living in now is preparing us for the Cosmic Reality?"

Yes, and when you learn how to use your spiritual PC properly, you will understand that you are not the computer itself (the body), but all the valuable stuff it contains.

Though you may often have to scandisk your belief drive and defrag your victim/death files, your cosmic web surfing will finally help you to see that fear is but a mere illusion when held up against your own Spirit's light and power. Your past inability to realize this has kicked you off-line, only to be rebooted into another life.

During your visits to the Earth site, you have created different screen names with the hope of reformatting your belief drive. But you have not taken the time to protect yourself against the hackers and viruses that have always made you crash. I know you can do better this time. I believe in you!

"And I believe in You!"

You must believe in your Self first, Keith, then it will be so much easier for you to believe in Me.

This is a precious time, not only for you, but for the evolution of the entire human race, because

I
Am
Here

to fulfill My promise etched on the hearts of all men and in all spiritual writings. Now is a time for everyone to make room within yourselves for Heaven on Earth.

"Will You please tell me how to manipulate energy so that I can make my life work better?"

Since you are a spiritual work in progress, you still perceive most things as made up of solid matter, not free energy. Your mind sees a chair as a chair, a table as a table and, until you change your mind, the chair will remain a chair and the table will remain a table. They cannot become anything else until you make that shift.

If you were to point to a chair and ask a Zen master, "What is that?" the answer you would get would most likely not match your own. He might tell you that he sees firewood or a stepladder.

"Why would he do that?"

Because that master, with his advanced way of seeing things, understands that the chair *could* become firewood, a stepladder or anything he needed it to be.

Since you are not yet similarly attuned, your mind still convinces you that you are looking at a chair, even though your eyes are seeing it as the radiated light it is.

Keith, if you like, I can explain the quantum mechanical physics involved, but what would you do with that?

"You know me well, not a thing. But could You explain it to me in laymen's terms?"

When the eyes see a chair, they take it in as radiated light, first through the lens, then the pupil, then on to the optic nerve and, finally, to the brain for analysis. The eyes instantly and literally pull the chair's matter apart strand-by-strand from the gross of it down to the nucleic particles of its atoms. You got that so far?

"I'm getting it."

Good, because getting the very simplicity of this idea is enough to help you succeed.

If you want to be able to transform that chair into a

table, you have to first know that the chair is not separate from you; you must see it as an extension of your own Self. Once you can see such dense matter as light particles, you will realize that your mind has indeed changed, that your own freewill has made a different choice and has anchored the "Everything is one" principle deep within. Will you let Me help you change your mind?

"Yes, please!"

Look at the chair across from where you are sitting now and let it reveal to you what it really is—radiated light. Now begin to look at it without judgment, as purely as the eyes do. Say to yourself, "There is no chair. What I see is light," then keep looking. Keep looking.

"Whoa!"

What is it, Keith?

"I saw little flashes of light all over it!"

What you saw were the random blips of energy that give the chair its form. Good job! You are finally beginning to retrain yourself to not be such a slave to the mind's opinions, but to let the mind become a catalyst for truth.

And the truth is that all matter is light compressed into specific vibrational forms decreed by the mind of the beholder. When you begin to see your own light in all things, you will then be able to transform your life, because your thought (or will) will be imbued with the power to create with mere intention. And do not forget to use My Love as your constant Source of power.

"Thank You for helping me see the 'light' about this 'matter'!" (laughing)

That is funny, Dear One! (joining in the laughter)

As a "matter" of fact, it is good to see that you can sometimes take things "lightly"!

"Why? Does that 'matter'?" (laughing harder)

Okay, that's good! Now "lighten up"! (laughing uncontrollably)

"Why? What's the 'matter'?" (also laughing uncontrollably)

Go "lightly" on Me, Beloved! (now guffawing)

"Phew...that felt great!" (smiling and letting out a big sigh of relief)

By laughing, you have just experienced one of the quickest ways to get to your enlightenment. So continue to laugh whenever you can. Fill your life with it. It is so good for you.

"Thanks! I'll definitely do that."

If you really want to manipulate energy, it would be wise for you to practice changing your mind about many areas of your life.

"So is that how Jesus changed water into wine, by changing His mind?"

There was a little more to it than that, but, yes, there was a shift. Jesus had a head start because He had a pure heart that enabled the Christ to quickly unfold within Him. Thus did Jesus the man become the Christ. When you have purified yourself, the same Divine Lotus Flower will blossom within your own heart and you, too, will be the Christ.

As you keep moving down life's timeline and up

towards consciousness, the Christ energy will help you, like It helped Jesus, to accomplish many things. Once you begin to make that kind of shift, you will find that physical reality and lighter realities can be experienced simultaneously. But your transition into lighter realities will depend solely upon you.

"I understand how it will work for me, but how will others move through this transition?"

Most people will go through it at a moderate pace. This will give them the time to understand what is happening to them more clearly, to work with it and to apply it. And once everyone really gets the hang of it, you and they may not only want to move in and out of alternate realities, but you may decide to manipulate physical matter to create some playthings to enjoy.

"Wow!"

On the other hand, when you all become aware that you are the Light that created your bodies, you can just as easily create new ones. (Not that you are not all perfect as you are.) It will be just as easy as choosing what clothes you want to wear.

Some of you might choose to move out of individuality altogether and merge with the Cosmic Sea of Divine Energy. And some will decide to continue living on the planet as your Higher Selves, further anchoring Heaven on Earth.

———— •◆• ————

Now that I have given you a glimpse of what is to come,

let us get back to the reality of the present.

As you work on becoming more aware of your light body, Spirit will stir dramatically and will let you know where you need to put more focus. And during such shifts, you will definitely begin to feel the heaviness of your body and the lightness of Spirit, depending on which way the shift scale has you tilting.

"I know what You're talking about — I live this dynamic daily!"

This bouncing body-to-Spirit dynamic is just what you *want* to have happen in order to take those out of body journeys, as you call them.

"So should my focus bounce back and forth between both?"

Try to balance them by making appropriate adjustments within yourself.

"But how?"

That is something I cannot tell you. That is something you must figure out for yourself. But what I can tell you is that all the tools you need you already have.

Here is an example of how to use them. If you want to go to Hawaii, picture in your mind's eye everything about it: its beaches, palm trees, coconuts, hula dancers and so on. These details will pinpoint your search. And if you do it right, before you know it, you will be sunning yourself on one of those beaches, holding a coconut cocktail in your hand, with hula girls and palm trees swaying nearby.

Inducing these experiences whenever you want to will take some practice but, over time, launching and landing will be as easy for you as driving an automobile.

"So is this the same as traveling through the stargates You mentioned before?"

No, but the intention is. I used the PC analogy earlier to help you get to the cosmic knowledge that will enable you to have those cosmic experiences you like so much. Here, we are talking about the fun you can have by roaming through the different dimensions and parallel realities of Earth.

"I'll work on both!"

Good, because this is what *all* your work is for—so you can free yourself to enjoy the cosmic playground I have created. Sounds like fun, does it not?

"Yes, it sure does!"

Keith, I know that My coming to you and telling you about how to "get out" has been a dream come true. You must feel some sort of relief.

"I do, but I have so many more desires, and they frustrate me because I can't seem to make those dreams a reality."

Know that your desires are not floating around in your mind just to tease you. I, the Gardener, have planted these seeds and it is I who encourages you to cultivate and harvest them. If you truly want your dreams to blossom, I say to you: "Seek ye first the Kingdom of God within you, and His Righteousness; and all these things shall be added unto you." (John 14:20)

Dreams manifest like this:

Giver→Receiver
Father→Mother
Unmanifest→Manifest

After a farmer plants seeds into his fertile field, he never disturbs them by digging them up to see if they are germinating. He does not have to. He knows that soon enough sprouts will emerge from the soil, and soon enough his garden will yield a bountiful harvest. All the while, he is humbled by the potential that lies within each seed.

Such is My relationship to you as Father, Farmer, Giver of seed.

A wife takes her husband's seed deep into her womb and conceives. It is then that the Universal Intelligence begins to move from the causal realm of the unmanifest to the physical world of the manifest. It is then that the Cosmic Body assembles all the parts necessary to bring a child into the world.

When the wife discovers she is with child, her joy and excitement overflow because she realizes that she has been given one of My greatest gifts. She knows that, soon enough, the child will be with her in the physical world, so she trusts the process, all the while going about her daily routine. In just nine months, when My fruit has ripened within her, another precious being begins its life on Earth.

Such is My relationship to you as Mother, Recipient, Bringer of harvest.

God is Life—Life is God.

From the unmanifest→manifest with simple intent. Is that simple or what?

"I'd say that's pretty simple!"

Simple it can be for you, too, when you live your life like the farmer and expectant mother—when you plant your seeds and turn your life over to God, then go about your day-to-day, all the while bringing your new life into being. Simple it can be when you have trust and patience. It is then that you can expect miracles.

"You're such a poet!"

I have My moments.

This book is a perfect example of somethingness from nothingness. Where do you think all this information comes from?

"Nothingness?"

Yes! And, is there not a book being born right before your very eyes?

"Yes, we are working on one, but it sure is taking a lot longer than nine months!"

That is what you think, My Divine Child. For even though you have been living in a time-space continuum, in eternity our book has already been written.

When you arrived on Earth, I gave you the freewill to write our book whenever you wanted to. But along the way, you have often chosen fear and this is what has kept you from getting it done. It has been your need for control and your doubt that have always hindered you.

Let us take a closer look at 'Freewill' as well as other

definitions that will clarify things a bit more.

Free

Not under control or power of another.

Able to act without arbitrary control or restriction.

Liberation.

Will

DESIRE, WISH: as DISPOSITION, INCLINATION <where there's a ~ there's a way>.

APPETITE, PASSION: CHOICE, DETERMINATION. Something desired; especially: a choice or determination of One having authority or power.

The act, process, or experience of willing: VOLITION.

Mental powers manifested as wishing, choosing, desiring, or intending.

A disposition to act according to principles or ends.

The collective desire of a group <the ~ of the people>

The power of control over One's own actions or emotions.

Intention

What one intends to do or bring about. The
object for which a prayer, mass, or pious act is
offered. Having the mind, attention, or will concentrated on something or some end or
purpose <~ on their work> a process or manner of healing of incised wounds. Concept;
especially: a concept considered as the product of attention directed to an object of
knowledge. Synonym: Intention, Intent,
Purpose, Design, Aim, End, Object, Objective,
Goal. Goal means what one intends to accomplish or attain. Intention implies little more than
what one has in mind to do or bring about
<announced his intention to marry>. Intent
suggests clearer formulation or greater deliber-
ateness <the clear intent of the statute>.

Attention

The act or state of attending esp. through
applying the mind to an object of sense or
thought. A condition of readiness for such
attention involving esp. a selective narrowing
or focusing of consciousness and receptivity.

You have the freewill to align yourself with the Good,
the Perfect, the Infinite. You also have the freewill to listen
to your ego ramble on. But if spiritual liberation is what you
truly desire, then you have to reach beyond your percep-

tion's grasp, beyond the practical, beyond the rational. For
your heart to burst open, you have to strive for the unfath-
omable. Love yourself as I do, Keith, and expand!

> While you grow,
>> for as long as it takes,
>>> and when you are ready,

I

Am

Here.

So, relax and enjoy your stay on Earth.

"Okay, I will, because I really enjoy living here."

Yes, I know. And if you want to continue to indulge your
humanness — to not come Home right now — go right
ahead. Believe Me, you will have another crack at it and so
will the many others who are not completely finished with
their spiritual development. But let Me remind you that
before you can board the Soul Train to Ascensionville, all
your karma must be resolved.

"I want to come aboard Your train, but something inside
me still makes me feel I don't deserve such liberation. Why
do I continue to carry guilt around when I know how completely useless it is?"

There is a part of you that still believes you are due
some punishment for your bad actions; it is this that holds
you back and makes you feel unworthy. When you feel this
way...

"Pardon me, I don't mean to interrupt, but sometimes it seems as though two entities are fighting over me. What's so tough is that I don't know which to listen to because when I reflect on the things I've done, sometimes the guilt kicks in. Other times, I say to myself that I will rise above it and do better. What can I do to be more consistent?"

As I was going to say before you stopped Me, just keep on praying and meditating.

"But I do both everyday."

Do you pray and meditate about this ongoing struggle of yours?

"Hardly ever."

Well, there you have it. Look, I know, I *absolutely* know, what it is like to live in duality because I watch all of you as you make your choices and then have to deal with their consequences. I know it is not easy. But the truth is that these are your choices:

You can live by Spirit's guidance or by human rationale.
You can live in trust or live with anxiety and desperation.
You can choose universal knowledge or planetary ignorance.
You can invite peace and Love into your heart
or hold anger and fear in your gut.

Dear One, the duality that troubles you can end at any time because you have already evolved enough to realize how much judging yourself the way you sometimes do has blocked your path to wholeness. But it is not only you, Keith. Most of the world lives in judgment. There are individuals who cast their judgment upon groups, groups who cast judgment upon other groups, groups who cast judgment upon individuals, individuals who cast judgment upon other individuals and individuals who cast judgment upon themselves. In all this judging, who is right?

"I wish I knew!"

Judging this and judging that. If I were a judgmental god as many claim, I would judge you for your judging and do away with all of you. Then no one would be left to judge!

"Why do we judge others so much? Is it so we can feel better about ourselves?"

Of course, but there are other reasons as well.

Many judge because they feel they have to peg irresponsible behavior in others as a way to stay detached from their folly. They are just calling a spade a spade.

And then there is the big one: people who think they must judge someone else's way of life on *My* behalf, as if they know who I would save and who I would toss away like yesterday's newspaper. I find it quite amusing when people assume that I share their opinions.

If I were to use right and wrong as My means of judgment, I could find many reasons to preserve some of the so-called bad and discard some of the so-called good amongst you. Indeed, I could find enough reasons to discard the physical universe altogether and start all over again. Just one tap on My DELETE button and that would be that! But what would be the point of such a judgmental approach?

"You're asking *me*?"

190

Yes, you!

"Why?"

Why not?

"But I thought that You were the One with all the answers."

Another belief! Answers to what? How short your memory is, Keith. Earlier I said that there are no questions. Now I say that there are no answers. How can there be? Questions and answers are the same. Either both exist or both do not. I live in the do not. You live in the do.

"You've got to be joking!"

Now that you mention it . . . Knock, knock . . .

"Oh no . . . You're not going *there?* Oh well, I'll bite . . . who's there?"

No body!

"And what's Your point?"

Perhaps there is no point. And that is what makes the joke so humorous.

"Oh, I see what You mean. That's why You find it so amusing when people judge, because there is no point to it at all."

Bingo! And you said you did not want to play My game with Me.

"I do, I do!"

I see that you have gained some enlightenment from My attempt at humor. So now you understand that if there is no knock-knock, there can be no light bulb moment, and that is no joke! The point is to not take life so seriously — to let go and have a good time — to laugh even when the joke is on you like it is now. Only those who have no sense of humor have a hard time getting life's joke — that the

191

meaning of life is the meaning that you give it. Get it?

"I got it! Uh, I mean that I think I've been got!"

Okay, as they say at rehearsal—one more time. Same joke—but this time, you start it.

"Okay. Knock, knock!"

Who's there?

"Keith."

Keith who?

"Umm..."

Confused?

"Darn, Ya got me again!"

Maybe, and until you do get it, whenever that may be, I await your response to life's ultimate riddle.

"I think I've got one now!"

What? (chortling) You actually think you may have an answer? Ah, yet again the joke is on you, Beloved. The ultimate punchline is that there is no right response—none whatsoever! You must pay closer attention, Keith. As I just said, *life is the meaning that you give it!* Could this be one of those times when you might decide to laugh at yourself?

"Okay, okay, I give up! What does all this have to do with judgment?"

When you are not laughing, check yourself, because you just may be judging. We got a little sidetracked because I simply wanted to show you how you were judging where our conversation was going—how you thought something was wrong with it that needed to be fixed.

"That's one more window of wisdom You have opened for

me! So, have *You* ever used judgment?"

I have never seen a flaw in anything. I see only perfection in what I have done, am doing and will do. There is a fine line between judgment and Creation. Those who dwell on the judgment side are seeing the world through their own imperfections and are keeping themselves separate from all that is already Perfect.

I do not create then judge. I use judgment *while* I create so that there is no need to use it later. I do it right the first time—even in My creation of you.

Beloved, do you think I created you so that I could one day judge your behavior and thus judge you?

"Not anymore I don't."

Ah, but many do. How could I ever grant you your freedom if I had to spend My time judging all six billion+ of you? The process would be never-ending and I would be so stressed out that My spiritual breakdown would be inevitable. Sound familiar?

"It sure does! But, as usual, I have another question. Is there such a thing as Judgment Day?"

Yes, but it is not I who will be the judge. As I said before, it is you who have been and always will be the judge of yourself. When your human death happens, you can expect to be shown your whole life from beginning to end. The question is, how do you judge yourself now and how will you judge yourself then? And is there really a difference between the two?

"I guess there isn't."

Do you feel that you deserve Love now, Beloved? Will

193

you accept it? Will you show yourself mercy? I am posing these kick-start questions to get you to move through your lingering fear about Me before that inevitable day, so that you can avoid repeating the same mistakes in your next reality. Because even though you may have some residual belief in a judgmental god, I assure you that judgment does not exist in Me!

I say to all: Whosoever continues to hold on to judgmental beliefs will find their lives filled with much needless effort and wasted energy. Your precious time on Earth will be spent in slavery!

LISTEN, MY CHILDREN OF THE LIGHT ETERNAL

You are embodiments of the Divine.
You are repositories of never-ending Bliss.
Your hearts are shrines to the Divine.
The whole of nature is your playground,
And all things in it are your playthings.
Regard yourselves as free,
as Masters of the universe.

*There are no strings attached
to My Earth experiment—
you are not marionettes!*

UNCONDITIONAL LOVE

You may ask why I do not solve the world's problems.

The answer: I do address them, but not by waving My Hand to remove them, for that would only negate My Unconditional Love, the Love that allows everything to be just as it is.

If I were to step in and immediately solve the calamities that you have created, all actions, development and evolution would stop and, if a greater need should arise, all of Creation would collapse with its Law of Cause and Effect in place.

The solutions you seek will come about when everyone becomes willing to be stripped of all that is impure and to be rebuilt into conscious beings. Only then will you be able to rise above your troubles and create a world of love, peace and unity.

*The world is in its predicament
not because of what God has made of man,
but because of what man has made of himself!*

———————•◆•———————

Unconditional

Without conditions or reservations; Absolute.

Absolute

Not limited, unconditional.

Entire, Pure.

I ask you to absorb these two definitions for they best describe My demeanor and the manner in which I conduct all My "business." My entire existence is based on the principle of allowance that gives you the freewill to choose your life, reality and destiny.

Some of the world's religions do not approve of, nor do they live by, the basic principles you are finding within this book. Their framework is one of right and wrong. They claim to know everything that "pleases" Me and everything that "disappoints" Me.

If I judged you as they believe I do, I would be a slave, at humanity's mercy, influenced by your behavior. As if My Reality could *ever* be influenced by what you do!

"I guess some people are so busy creating God in *their* own image that they just can't imagine You creating us in Yours."

Yes, but that view is misleading because it implies that I am a god of jealousy and control—that I use My muscle to bully everyone into doing what I want them to do and if they do not, I deny them their trip up to Heaven.

But I do not do that. As I observe the human condition, I look upon everyone with compassion. I especially support the efforts of all who are trying to right themselves because they want to, not because of some threat of a possible hellfire and brimstone manipulation by Me. That is the preciousness of freewill; you either use it or you do not. There are no strings attached to My Earth experiment —you are not marionettes!

The irony of it is that your freewill has cost you all a bundle. You yourself, Keith, have paid a huge price because of the "poor" choices you have made.

"I know, I know, but what is it that I'm still not doing correctly?"

You still sometimes choose to let your ego dictate your life. That is what has kept you snared in a neurotic trap set by no one but yourself.

"Maybe I'm not exactly clear about what the ego is."

Most are not, so I shall explain by first giving the definition, then follow that up with further insight.

Ego

The self; the individual as aware of himself.

The part of the psyche which controls the impulses of the identity.

Your ego is made up of all the fear-based thoughts you have about yourself and the world around you. An ego-driven person tends to gloat and boast to others, trying to create a false impression that he or she is happier than he/she really is. Do you think I fit into this category?

"God, no! Not at all! Do *I* fit into this category?"

Not so much in terms of gloating or boasting, but rather, in the way you let things come between you and the life you desire and deserve.

"So how do *You* do it?"

There is no fear in Me. And, because I am Self-fulfilled, I have no need to project false light to try to convince anyone of anything. I am happy just the way I am. I accept all that I have brought forth and I see nothing I would change. Does that answer your question?

"Yes, it does. What You're saying is that when we choose to become enlightened, Heaven comes down to us."

Yes, and it is just a matter of time, for time is the space between those who take the spiritual path now and those who put it off. If you extract time and space from the equation, what are you left with?

"Just one big enlightenment?"

Bang! You got it. Welcome to eternity. Take your shoes off and make your Selves at Home!

"I need a moment!"

What is the matter, Keith?

"That hit me hard!" (teary-eyed)

Just wait until you *really* get it! Let Me know when you are ready to continue, Dear One.

"I'm ready." (still sniffling a little)

Let us look at the way both types of people I just mentioned conduct their lives.

Conscious practitioners spend at least a little time each day reflecting on their lives — day by day, week by week, month by month, year by year. This lets them see their patterns and gives them accurate clues as to why they are where they are. Their self-reflection is the springboard that lets them make the best choice at any God-given moment. And, since they are always looking to find a better way to flow with the universal current, they take full advantage of the coincidences that happen in their lives (the synchronicity) and use them to decode signals from the Higher Self. As a result, their quality of life is enhanced.

By aligning with the universe's forces, spiritual practitioners are able to tap into them for the betterment of themselves and the rest of mankind. Their road to God is dramatically shortened to only a few lives because they have chosen to learn while they live life and are not relying solely on the life overview you have all come to expect when you die.

In contrast, unconscious practitioners live the same routine day after day. They never reflect on their past but, instead, they dwell upon it, all the while fearing the future. They are rarely open to receive any of the miracles that could sweeten and ease their lives, so they work, work, work to gain the money they think will enhance them.

Unconscious practitioners are only concerned with what they can get while they are living. They mostly learn about Spirit during their death transitions, when they are shown how much the choices they made affected everyone in their most recent life experience as well as themselves.

But even though they may have learned from their life overview, it does not mean that they are apt to reach for a higher place in their next incarnation. Their ongoing procrastination will cause them to hack away at life until they experience something of great enormity that motivates them towards Spirit or until they choose the spiritual path of their own volition.

> *Whenever,*
> *whether now or later,*
> *you will be back and I will be waiting—*
> *waiting for you to walk into your divinity,*
> *regain your Divine Consciousness,*
> *merge with the expanding universe*
> *and create a life of Love.*

Understand that whether or not you live a spiritual life now makes no difference to Me whatsoever.

"It doesn't? Why do You say that?"

Because however people live, My Love for them does not waver.

"That's good to know. But I still waver, and I sometimes worry that my wavering might cause me to hurt myself."

You mean your body? Remember, your body is not what you are. You are Spirit—indestructible, impervious to fear, disease and death. If you *could* hurt your Self, Dear One, I assure you that I would become the strict parent some religions make Me out to be and I would keep you from doing so.

"That's why some religions preach how strict You are and say that fear is the devil, disease is deadly and death is the end. That's what makes them think that it actually bothers You for people to be the way they are."

Is that the thought that just came to you?

"Yes." (pleased with himself)

But I sent that "I-mail" to you eons ago! You must be using an older modem to log on to My Innernet. What? About 28k, you think? (laughing)

(Keith laughing)

I am just being light with you. Seriously though, what you just said only furthers My point about why it has taken you eight years to write our book. By falsely identifying yourself as the body, you are still keeping yourself from getting valuable information when you really could use it. Yes, you still sometimes look in the mirror, see your reflection and believe that that is you.

Can you understand why, in your earlier years, believing that you were only your body gave you no choice but to assume that the lights go out forever when you die? Because of your limited knowledge, you were convinced that there is no life beyond physical life, so you feared death. But once you began to have some sense of yourself as the spirit, you exchanged that fear with a fear that death would not bring everlasting life, but only everlasting torment.

Fear is what has slowed you down and caused you to feel inadequate. It has also led you to believe that there is no hope for your future. But, as you have now found out, because of your intentions to transcend your fears, I have been helping you get back on track to that blissful life you long for.

"Yes, You have, but what about those who don't show any intention for transcendence? Do You help them as well?"

I love everyone dearly, even the ones who let My efforts to touch them slip by unused.

Time will come and time will go.
People will live happily,
only to die and move to a higher level.

Time will come and time will go.
People will live sadly, only to die
and have to do it over again until they get it right.

———— ◆ ————

As you continue to expand, you may notice a deepened sense of compassion that causes you to be concerned about the loved ones around who you are having troubles.

"I know that feeling well. And I know the next thing You're going to say is that I should just try to sit back and let their lives happen."

Yes, that would be best right now.

"That's so hard for me to do!"

I do it.

"But You are God!"

And you are not?

"Well, yes, You have taught me that I am, but . . . "

If you really want to help someone you care about, you do not have to do anything for them. You can get the job done just by being an anchor for Love like Me.

"But I like to help and share what I know."

Yes, you go at it with all that you have. And how many have taken you up on your offer?

"Some have, but when it comes right down to it, most don't seem to want it after all. Why's that?"

Two reasons: their rebellious nature may keep them from receiving your "help," or their spirit might reject it simply because your "help" would undermine their growth. This is not the outcome we want now, is it? Whatever the reason, their present circumstance is one which they and they alone must figure out.

Know that I hear their cries, too, for days, months and even years on end. But I, too, must step back, for if I "played god" that would stop their evolution and rob them of the freewill that I have freely given them.

"I don't get it, so You just do nothing?"

I help all the time, but many have not done the work required for them to recognize it when it does show up. Nevertheless, they try to make the best of their lives using what they little faith they do have. Over time, some may lose that faith or become agnostics, even atheists. Yet, even though they are trapped in difficulty, I love them just as much as the ones who have become illumined.

"You always make things sound so simple. Are we that blind?"

Let Me put it this way: When, at last, the human race comes to see that Love is the Beginning and the End, that is when it will see how its fear has served no purpose whatsoever; and that, no matter what, it is Love that does and will prevail.

"So fear is just resistance to Your Will?"

Yes. If someone lives in constant fear, they are swimming against the natural flow of the universal stream. Actually, fear is the stone that tries to hold back the stream, but that only causes rapids to rise up which must be ridden out with care.

"I have steered my raft through those waters way too many times by not making decisions based on Spirit. But I've noticed that as soon as I turn to You, I get back in the flow and everything seems to smooth right out."

So you have incorporated the two key components— intending to get back in the flow and knowing where to look to do that. Good for you. But there are those who will continue riding those rapids their whole lives—who will never choose to "live in God" nor "let" God live in them.

"Are You talking about atheists? Are they 'doomed' if they don't convert, as some believe?"

The fact is, anyone who lives righteously can row their boat ashore. It is not about the thoughts that lie in one's head. It is about the actions one does. What would make an atheist any different from someone who believes in Me and does not live that belief?

"I guess there would be no difference."

I am not a hypocrite, Keith. Just because people may not believe in Me does not mean that they are condemned. If that were the case, it would mean that I have no faith that one day they will reciprocate My Love.

But those who are not atheists—those who claim to have faith—may still, in one breath, say that I am a loving God and, in the next, say that I am judgmental and controlling. It is no small wonder that they fear Me. They do not realize how inconsistent their beliefs are or how ironic it is that, when they return from a near-death experience, they swear on My name that they have gone to hell.

"The sound of that is just so hideous to me!" (shuddering)

Why do you shudder, Beloved? They went to no such place. Where they went was deep into their own fear—*that* is their hell! I ask you, who is the real hypocrite here? And why is it so hard for people to believe in an absolute loving God only?

"I suppose many think that's what a devil would want — for us to believe that he doesn't actually exist."

Yes, and people hold on to that idea of hell with all tenacity, thinking that if they do not believe in a devil, their afterlife consequences will be even worse. What can possibly be worse?

"I can only assume that they can't see it any other way."

You are correct. They cannot entertain a sense of wonderment about a higher realm as the first option because they believe they deserve condemnation. They beat themselves up with a guilt bat, administering the punishment they feel they are due—and that sets even more karma into motion. To live this way is self-abuse.

"Does guilt have a purpose?"

Guilt serves the sole/Soul purpose of letting someone know they are in poor choice mode. If people would just slow down and begin to pay attention to the thoughts they are thinking, they would be able to differentiate between the low ones and the high ones, and they would see how religiously choosing the higher ones can only help them climb up the spiritual (Spirit-ritual) ladder.

People who live in a constant state of guilt are not at all happy about the inevitable idea of death because they fear what they think they are going to face when they die.

"Well, if this is how they think their afterlife is going to be, why is it they do nothing to change the bad behavior that they think will land them there?"

Good question. And I have an answer that just might surprise you. Deep within everyone, the truth resonates that hell does not exist, but many have not yet found a way to unlearn the false programming that consumes them.

Anyone who truly believes that if they are "bad" they will be condemned, should find that prospect enough of a deterrent to stop their supposed wrongdoings. That alone should scare the "hell" out of them! Seriously, it should. Right?

"I agree."

It is no wonder so many of you are so head over heels confused. You are trying to find peace using a thought process that is outer-to-Inner, fear-over-Love, hell-over-

Heaven. I ask any who actually believe that *God* behaves like *they* do: Why do *you* not behave like *Me?*

"I guess it's hard to duplicate Your behavior if, within ourselves, we don't know You well enough to do so."

Very well said.

I say to My Loved Ones who are reading these words and are still living back-to-front: reverse your thinking now. For if you continue letting your ego dictate how you live, the entire drama of what I have just explained will unfold before you and you will find yourself in this same spot in your next life, having to do it all over again.

If you are living without a clue about what is happening in this period of change, without a clue about who you really are and why you are really here, heed the following:

You are being guided now
in small steps you can manage.
In due course,
Love will expand into your lives
until you are consumed by Love
and become Love and, in Love,
merge as One with God
who is Love Itself.

*Questions are good,
for they can only lead you
to your answers.*

*Rest assured that you will
only get answers that reflect
the quantity of Soul quality
you have invested in your
questioning.*

Thought, Feeling and Reality

At present, humanity is living the book of the Bible called Revelation. If you see its message from the perspective of "My time is nearly up, so I'd better repent and begin to behave myself," you believe that what you have done and continue to do without considering God will surely result in judgment. If you choose to think thusly, your reality will reflect your spiritual status.

———•◆•———

As the Earth becomes enveloped in higher energies, whoever does not take full advantage of the opportunity for balance that this situation presents will surely regret it. Mark My Word, when negative things begin to happen to you, you will not find it at all pleasing and, unlike in the past, this time you will have no choice but to respond!

211

The fact of the matter is, the longer you avoid dealing with your unresolved issues, the more difficult they will become to resolve. Your best move is to stay ahead of the game or, at the very least, to stay on top of things.

"How do we do that?"

First, put My Love into your daily practice by meditating and by following your heart.

Second, integrate all I have spoken of since the beginning of this transmission and apply those teachings to your life.

And third, realize that one Supreme Loving God moves everything in the universe.

Acknowledging My Presence in these ways will help you to heighten your awareness and will empower you to improve your life. I guarantee that you will love what unfolds.

Now, back to Webster's for clarity.

Intuition

Quick and ready insight. Immediate apprehension or cognition; knowledge or conviction gained by intuition.

The power or faculty of attaining to direct knowledge or cognition without evident rational thought and inference.

Feeling

An awareness; consciousness; an emotion; a premonition.

"I love using my intuition to help others, but I worry about whether I'm using it to its fullest whenever someone asks me for spiritual guidance. It bothers me that, at any time, I could be wrong in the readings I give."

Not to worry, My Beloved. When you question your accuracy, it only shows you how much work you still have to do. At the same time, it shows Me how responsible you want to be.

Though your concern about having to be "right" may cause you to veer into the wrong lane every once in awhile, good driver that you have become, you are now learning how unimportant it is to be right. Besides, did it ever occur to you in the readings you give, that when you feel you might be wrong, it is exactly what your questioner needs to hear for their growth? Indeed, maybe you are right after all.

"I never thought of it that way. So there's really no difference between being right and being accurate?"

I shall tell you the difference. Those who believe it matters how people perceive them and who always need to be right are following an agenda that is ego-based and outer driven. But the desire to be accurate requires an inner discipline and has no agenda except the highest good.

"That's my goal, but I still have some questions surrounding this subject."

That is good, for questions can only lead you to your answers. Rest assured that you will only get answers that reflect the quantity of Soul quality you have invested in your questioning.

Now *I* have a question. Since I have done My best to tell you of the joy, prosperity and intuitive powers that await you, why do you still settle for the ordinary? Do you think that is all you can have—all you deserve?

"I've thought and felt that my life's been ordinary for so long — at least until recently."

Yes, you have stayed in that comfort zone of yours, only to find that nothing ever seems to change. No wonder you have wondered, "Why am I not happy and at peace like I know I could be?"

The reason is that you are still thinking too much and not feeling enough. For you to ever know your own capacity for Love, you must learn how to stay out of your believing head and to steer your life only with your knowing heart.

But I caution you, Keith, as you effort to become more of a "feeler," you may find yourself thinking about your past times of suicidal despair—those times when you totally shut off your ability and willingness to feel anything.

"I really don't like visiting that place!"

Ah, but it is the place you need to get to because that is where your unaddressed issues are buried—the ones that have caused you so much grief, the ones that must be changed for you to reach peace.

Just think about the girls and women you have dated— from one to the next to the next. Though their names have been different, the relationships have all played out pretty much the same—fraught with angst-filled drama and, inevitably, ending in a breakup.

How pleased I am that you are beginning to see at last that acknowledging any pattern is the halfway point to change. The other half, as you also know by now, is to keep on doing the actual work — to totally commit to your new ways by resisting every temptation to go back to the old. Hold yourself steady as you would a magnifying glass to the sun — a little longer each time until a clearer image of your path is burned into your consciousness. Know that just because the sun sets, it does not mean that your day's work is done. Changing your life patterns is a 24/7 job.

One more thing you have not yet learned as you have played life over and over is how assigning guilt to someone only nullifies your own power and leaves both of you with hopeless, angry thoughts. So here is another guideline for you: Each time you point the finger of blame at someone else, you might as well be pointing it at yourself!

With My guidance, maybe this time you will be able to stay centered in your heart so that when your karma does show up again, you will not do what you have done before — *re*act. Maybe this time you will do your best to forgive and love just because you can.

Dearest, what you and everyone should want to be overcome by is that "Aha! I've got it!" feeling, and you get that when you come from Love, not from fear. You will not believe how much easier it is to carry the Divine Torch of Enlightenment through life than it is to bear the burden of ignorance, fear and pain.

"So what should I be paying attention to?"

Your feelings, Beloved, because how you feel will let

you gauge the thoughts that you are choosing. As long as you stay in your mind, the outside world can influence you to make more bad choices, and that will only delay your time of peace.

"But what's out there seems so real."

Yes, the physical world is temptingly convincing. But when will you realize that it does not exist for you if you are not there to acknowledge it? If you keep on investing yourself in the world outside which, by its very nature, is forever in a state of flux, how can you expect to ever become still enough to find My Peace within yourself?

"Who knows?"

I do.

"Really. Then tell me, when?"

When you choose to, Beloved, when you choose to.

You create your reality in every moment by your own perceptions, judgments and actions.

Peace is a state of Mind.
Bliss is a state of Heart.
Heaven is a state of Being.

Again, back we go to the basics. "The Kingdom of God cometh not with observation, neither shall they say, Lo here or, lo there! for, behold, the Kingdom of God is within you." (Luke 17:20–21)

Scripture offers this message to one and all. Still, many consider Me to be a separate reality and never let themselves see the connection between us.

Can you understand why people are not willing to change their thinking? Like you, most live with deeply rooted beliefs, reinforced from their past and past lives. More than likely, this explanation does not surprise you because you know what it has taken for you to move through your own "I am separate from God" belief. But the fact remains that, for the world to actually become the Kingdom written about in this passage of Scripture, everyone must do the requisite spiritual work.

The good news is that the truth process has already begun. It is not difficult to find malfeasance of all kinds revealing itself. Governments are being exposed for what they do; officials of some religious denominations now face challenges because they have chosen to sweep their clergymen's misdeeds under the rug; schools are full of too little learning and too much violence; and the economy, well, it seems that many of the institutions that the world assumed were stable are showing some definite signs of breaking down.

I tell you again that if humanity were in alignment with the Divine Will, it would not be in its present condition. But rest assured, this "condition" will be corrected early in the new millennium. That is when the entire world will find itself submerged in absolute God change. And that is when it will become mandatory for everyone to question everything you believe to be true. As you all meditate upon the enigma of God, you will have no choice but to reexamine what you think to be Divine.

"What will help to restore order?"

When everyone efforts to replace their concepts of right and wrong with a deliberate intent to live peacefully at all costs—that alone will help the world to regain its equilibrium.

Can you tell Me whose opinion is truly right amongst the six or so billion of you? One's right is always someone else's wrong. Why, even in your lifetime, you have all been witness to diplomatic debates that have escalated from disagreement to argument, argument to conflict and, before you knew it—to war!

But the use of military might is not an option anymore. The only way to restore order is for everyone to see everything as I see it—with Love, in Love, as Love.

"I really like the simplicity of what You've just said about seeing all things 'with Love, in Love, as Love.' That's nice."

Just imagine what would happen if all the world's citizens truly desired peace! Imagine the quiet that would blanket your minds and the globe if all the bickering stopped. Why, peace could come to pass overnight! But, needless to say, the guidance everyone needs to make that happen cannot possibly be heard when the voices of right and wrong are still making such a racket.

"Yeah, sometimes those voices are so loud that they almost drive me crazy."

When that happens, it is just the devil and angel you talked about earlier actively enticing you to come their way. It is obvious that the devil image on your shoulder is devilish, but are you absolutely sure that the angel on your other shoulder is not the same devil in disguise?

I tell you that these two tempters are only capable of whispering incorrect choices in your ear. The correct choice, the *only* choice, for you to heed is the one that encourages you to use the Divine Principles and Spiritual Laws to move through the duality of right and wrong.

"I do all I can to live by them but when I do, fear sometimes wells up inside of me."

Fear of what?

"You." (slightly embarrassed)

Me?

"Yes, but it's on a level I don't think I understand yet."

Oh yes you do, Keith! You know that your fear comes from what you were taught about Me long ago. Still, that does not mean I am that way. I am not about the praise and punishment that you were subjected to as a child. Do not forget that you are the one who has chosen to live in this world of duality that mirrors everything you are. Once you decide to take full responsibility for creating your experience, you will be afraid of nothing.

Take a moment now and imagine you are sitting by a small, still pond. You look into it and see your face looking back at you. You try to touch your reflection, but as your hand skims the water, the image disappears. When that happens, you feel certain that what you have seen is an illusion. So you reach up to touch your face, confident that your tangible body is real and your reflection is not.

But do not be fooled, Keith. Only your experience of that experience—or any experience—is what can be considered real. And, no matter what you believe about anything, all you will ever see is your self/Self.

"Please tell me more about how my thoughts and feelings work?"

There are no neutral thoughts—only love-based ones or fear-based ones. Love-based thoughts are permissive and cast no judgment. Fear-based thoughts do just the opposite.

If you imagine you are listening to the radio and you liken your thoughts to its many stations and your feelings to its volume, what happens when you crank that volume up?

"The music I've chosen gets very loud."

Yes, depending on the station you select (your love thoughts or guilt thoughts), life's radio will either play you a love song or the blues.

We will be right back after a word from our sponsor.

"YOU ARE NOW TUNED IN TO STATION *WGOD* —YOUR *TRUE* SOUL MUSIC STATION!"

"That's very funny!"

Yes, it is, but it does show you exactly how your judgments (thought) and convictions (feelings) manifest your reality. So, if you want your life to be filled with beautiful, uplifting music, you must first feel the joy that you know having what you desire will bring to you, and then allow that feeling to take form in your mind's eye. The correct sequence you must employ in order to create deliberately is feeling→thought, not thought→feeling.

———————

There are countless millions—those who function using

the left side of their brains — who still require some proof before they can make any life-altering decisions. They are akin to Old World scientists because they think that if something cannot be seen then there must be nothing there. Their belief in such limitations explains the difficulty they have in obtaining what they desire. I ask you: Can you see Love under a microscope?

"It's impossible to do that, isn't it?"

Yes, but just because something cannot be seen does not mean it does not exist. Not understanding this is why most people's faith comes to a grinding halt.

The fact is, they end their search too soon. Most try a little of this, a little of that, and when nothing seems to happen, they say, "Well, I guess this is what I get." They sigh, "This is all I'm supposed to have." They lament, "Perhaps what I'm shooting for is impossible to achieve or maybe it does not exist at all." And then they give up entirely, never to try again.

"I can't tell You how many times I've done this myself."

That does not necessarily mean that you are looking in the wrong places. What it means is that you have the same lack of patience that's keeping everyone else so bamboozled. You must know that if you approach any situation with the attitude of "I will believe it when I see it," then you will never see it. If you believe that it will happen, eventually it will.

Now, let us say that you truly believe that what you desire will come to pass. If you wonder why nothing is happening, understand that this might mean that you are still too attached to the outcome. Or it could mean that you are looking for it to manifest in a particular way. If that last one is the case, you might well miss "it" when it shows up in another way entirely.

Trust Me, when the time is right for you to get what you have been wanting, I will come to you and whisper, "Pssst, over here"—and there it shall be!

"There's something else I want to ask You."

Sure. Go ahead.

"This morning I saw a program on the Discovery Channel about the Hubble telescope. It talked about how much science has learned. But what flashed through my mind as I was watching, was the 'PC' technique You taught me earlier and how it seems to be the better way to explore the universe."

It is common knowledge that when astronomers and other scientists look into deep space to study cosmic occurrences, they are witnessing the light from events that actually took place long ago. All their high-tech equipment might help prove some of their theories, but, without inner vision, these experts will stay unaware of what is *presently* taking place throughout the universe. As long as they remain in a spiritually myopic state, they will not be able to harness the power that true cosmic knowledge can bring.

On the other hand, spiritualists understand that Light is the product of a pure, enlightened consciousness, and so they dedicate their lives to achieving just that. The more they develop themselves and begin to consciously connect to the omnipresent Spirit, the more they are able to witness the grandeur of the universe here and now.

"So are You saying that Light has no velocity?"

None whatsoever. Light is everywhere at all times, or at no time, should I say. Just like a hologram, the whole is inherent in every fragment of Light throughout the entire cosmos. You might say that "God Cosmosis" is taking place everywhere.

Relativity

The quality or state of being relative; something that is relative.

The state of being dependent for existence on or determined in nature, value, or quality by relation to something else. Theory of the relative, rather than the Absolute. The interdependence of matter, time, and space: as developed by Albert Einstein in two separate theories, the theory includes the statements that: Motion is relative, not absolute; The velocity of light is constant; The mass of a body in motion varies with the velocity, space and time are interdependent and form a four-dimensional continuum.

One of the greatest minds in all of history belonged to Albert Einstein. His mission when he was on Earth was to present his Theory of Relativity to the world, a theory that prepares you for an even greater truth to come. Since that day is almost here, I shall give you a new formula, an updated one that takes into consideration the shifting and re-shifting that has taken place since his original one was proffered.

Einstein's formula said that nothing can go faster than the speed of light.

THE THEORY OF RELATIVITY

$$E = m c^2$$

where,

$$E = \text{energy}$$
$$M = \text{mass}$$
$$C = \text{light}$$

The new formula says that there is something faster than light, and that something is thought.

The difference between these two theories? This one states that slowly but surely, linear time is depleting.

THE THEORY OF REALITY

$$E = m c \frac{\pi}{\text{RELATIVITY}} \frac{\pi}{4}$$

where,

$$E = \text{energy: lifting}$$
$$M = \text{mass: manifesting energy}$$
$$C = \text{Light: omnipresent, with no velocity}$$

The π over RELATIVITY correlates to the quickening that is now taking place. RELATIVITY correlates directly to people—all the relative, personified spirits who use the primal force of *thought* to create and define reality, whether it be with clarity, knowing and intention, or with confusion, belief, opinions and judgment.

The π over 4 represents the "no time" factor that diminishes the space between your thoughts and the manifestation of reality—the window between what you think and what happens.

The number 4, in this case, is the numerical symbol that signifies the power of the whole that will move within you and permeate your emotional body as intense *feeling*, thus guaranteeing manifestation of the self/Self.

Thought

The act or process of thinking; reflection; meditation. The power of reasoning; intellect; imagination.

Through physics, Einstein's Theory of Relativity revealed to the world its linear→vertical thought-speed capacity. Now, as people become more aware that they are one, that very capacity will change exponentially.

"Whoa! Can You give me a little more insight here?"

Sure, Keith. I shall use math this time.

Before someone is exposed to math's principles, their thought processes proceed more or less on a linear level. Once they learn its basic applications, more advanced modalities of vertical thought begin to emerge. Their mental capacity increases as they master algebra, geometry, trigonometry and calculus. If they go on to study physics, quantum physics and metaphysics, they come to understand much more about the universe and how it functions.

But neither math's formulas nor its numbers are really that important. Math's real value lies in the expansion it brings to the minds of those who master it. Math offers a way for people to comprehend something "higher" than themselves.

Still using basic math, let us look at the foundation a child operates from. What concept does the child first learn?

"Mommy and Daddy?"

Yes, that is true, but I am speaking of numbers here. The number one is the very first concept a child learns. The child discovers who he/she is as *one* and interacts with the world using that awareness. Yes, children understand the universal primordial number before math ever comes into play, because it is the nature of the universe to operate from this premise.

Zero

Nothing; figure 0; point on a graduated instrument from which positive and negative quantities are reckoned.

Now for the concept of zero. Among zero's many Divine attributes are wholeness, balance, completion, union and, last but not least, eternity. Zero is the highest idea there is, but it is not very user-friendly, for it requires you to fully comprehend the idea of nothing or no-thing —God.

Notice that I said "idea," because zero is just that—not a number, but a concept. And until a system is in place that enables the collective mind to expand into whole thought, understanding the Divine will remain a challenge.

As with zero, the number one is a formidable number to realize. If you do not understand the concept of one, trying to comprehend numerical concepts such as millions, billions and trillions would only be putting the cart before the horse. Just know that if you continue to break everything down into bits, you will always find yourself living in a world of multiplicity and separation.

"God, my brain hurts!"

I know, that was a lot to absorb.

"Even though I'm pretty full, there's probably room for a little more."

Good, because we only have a little more to do today.

As we look to history, we learn of people who are now deemed to be "great," but who were regarded as quacks, crazies and troublemakers by their contemporaries during their time on Earth. Is it not ironic, Beloved, how these prodigies were only accepted after their lifetimes?

"Yes, but that doesn't surprise me."

Just about everything of value you use in your modern world was gifted to you by these so-called weirdos. I shall name but a few: Jesus, Franklin, Edison, Tesla and Einstein.

Not only were these geniuses (among others) divinely inspired, but they understood the One/Zero Principle, so they were able to make their great discoveries and thus better humanity.

"But many will object..."

Ah, Loved One, I already know what you are going to say. You want to know how Jesus can be included in the same category as those others. When people ask, just tell them I told you to say that greatness cannot be separated from what it essentially is — great. All of these "greats" have given you gifts to better your world.

It is your root fear
that first filters
the Soul's light.

The tools of understanding
are the only things
that will help you
break on through
to the other side.

SANDWICHED BETWEEN
GOD AND THE DEVIL

Fear contracts — Love expands.
Fear works from outside to inside;
Love, from inside to outside.

Fear is the taker; it draws everything into itself
and gives nothing.
Fear takes what it can when it can
to feed a hunger that can never be satisfied.
Fear creates judgment, which creates separation.

All that Love does is give. It nourishes Itself,
yet has infinite leftovers to offer everyone and everything.
Love is never hungry.
Love creates acceptance, which creates unity.
Love is a Fountain of Wealth that is endless, eternal.

———— ◆ ————

231

Fear

Anxiety and agitation caused by the presence of danger, evil, pain, etc. Dread; fright.

Awe; reverence. A feeling of uneasiness.

Once all of you see what your fears are doing to you, you will quickly kick the habit, because fear, like smoking, will eat away at you and cause your body to deteriorate, age and die.

"So why do we have fear?"

The reason is simple. When you left the Godhead to create your lives as individuals, for a brief moment you were vulnerable. It was then that those who cared not one iota about you, about Love, or about anything else, took the opportunity to impregnate you with whatever they could that would help them to always dominate.

"What's to stop the Luciferians from taking over the whole world?"

You and everyone like you! Since light always dispels darkness, once you all begin to use what you are learning, My Love will become part of your daily lives and they will simply disappear.

"Can You tell me when this is going to happen?"

As far as I can tell, 2017 is the year humanity will make that shift.

"You mean You don't know?"

How could I? This is your show! My prediction is based on what is likely to transpire from the choices everyone is making now.

"So if Heaven on Earth was a sure thing all along, why was the Luciferian interference allowed to happen at all?"

Because that is what I do—I *allow*. I assure you, Dear One, that in the course of what you perceive as time, Heaven on Earth *will* manifest, because My Will cannot be stopped by anything. But *you* can be stopped by your fear.

"So fear is what keeps us caught up in time?"

Yes, and until you consciously reunite with the eternal, where fear is non-existent, for you time will drag.

To help you see what I mean, I ask you to reflect now on the past and look into the future, focusing on the time you have shared and will share with loved ones.

The now moments you share with older relatives will one day become moments of your past. After your loved ones die, you can say that all those times you shared with them are your past-now moments.

You will have now moments with others in the future as well. Those times you will spend with people later on will be now-future moments.

Likewise, for future generations, you will be present in their past-now moments and so on. Throughout time, the only continuum is the *now*. And, as I said, not until you transcend your fear will you be able to know what I know and see time as I do.

"So time after time, I've spoiled my own chances to truly see?"

Right. The moment you let fear influence whatever matter is at hand, you can see nothing except what you fear.

For most people, a visit to the doctor or dentist causes the kind of anxiety that seems to make time last forever. On the other hand, when you are doing something you love, have you not noticed how time flies?

"Yes, why's that?"

Because you are focused on the joy such moments bring and, for that moment, you touch the eternal.

Remember what it was like when you worked those 9–5 jobs that you did not want to be at—how long your work days seem to last?

"I am glad that's a past-now moment!" (sighing a sigh of relief)

Have you noticed how some of your friends hate going to work, too? They could change jobs or career direction like you did and begin to live their passion, but most do not. Can you tell Me why?

"They're like I once was — they fear change or they are afraid of what other people might think of their quitting."

Right on both counts. Plus, they have a fear of lack. They think that nothing more satisfying, creative and/or financially rewarding will ever come their way. It is no wonder that life for them seems hopeless. Their problem is that they have become so tightly wrapped around their own drama that they fear the story they are living will never end. Some may even wish their lives were already over, but yet, not too soon, because they are still like you once were — afraid that, in death, the lights will go out forever.

But these perceptions are fiction! The truth: In the Book of Love—a work of non-fiction—your present lives are

SANDWICHED BETWEEN GOD AND THE DEVIL

sentences that will indeed end after a period. But then everyone will go on to live other life sentences that will form the paragraphs to eventually write the next chapter of My universal story.

"Where does our fear of death come from?"

Some fear death because they still hold a past life memory of how they once died. But for many, it is not about the fear of death, it is about regret—regret that they have not allowed themselves to actually live. Just look at how afraid you were to live fully, Keith, to really let go and have a good time. Do you not regret all the time you wasted?

"Yes, I sure do!"

You can bet that your regret directly relates to any fear of death you are still harboring. Perhaps you are like those who think that if they give up being afraid, their lives will only get worse. Humanity has become so comfortably mired in its fear quandary that it does not remember how to balance itself. You will only be able to discover the motivation and the kind of strength you need to face your fears head-on when you come together and make the effort to work things out. My Beloveds, it is time to lay your weary heads to rest.

"How can fear have such a hold on us?"

Fear keeps you believing that what is not there is actually there. It can take any form to validate you and your make-believe reality. Further, fear energy does not just disappear; it feeds upon itself in a never-ending loop until you equalize its frequency.

"Can You give me an illustration?"

Gladly. Do you mind if I use one of your own personal fears to do that?

"Uh...I guess not..." (reluctant)

On a beautiful spring night, you decide to take a walk around your neighborhood. Suddenly, out of nowhere, there appears a big barking dog.

Perception:	"Oh no! A dog!"
Judgment:	"Mean dog hurt me!"
Feeling:	"I'm afraid!"
Thought:	"What's my best move?"
Reaction:	"Run...
Intention:	...faster than the dog!"

"I suppose You think that's funny?"

And you do not?

"No, it's too real for me!"

When oh when will you release yourself from the fearful thinking that can only result in outcomes you do not want?

"When I choose to?"

There is no other way, Keith. Believing that there is something to be afraid of is what helps sustain the wall between you and your liberation. What do you think it will take to help you break on through to the other side?

"I guess I need a good power tool."

You already have it, Dearest, but you must put it to better use. One of the quickest ways for you to become a good Craftsman is to practice stretching the miniscule, silent space that resides between each thought.

"You mean meditation?"

Precisely.

"But I'm already doing that."

Yes, but doing it more would not hurt, because as soon as you can reach a deeper state than you have been able to get to before, the sooner you will find an even sweeter spot, a place where you can make peace with your lingering fears.

"Once I get there, then what?"

Invite those fears in, thank them and firmly tell them, "I no longer need you in my life — goodbye!" And know it to be so.

"But that sounds too easy."

And what is wrong with that? The Self has power to spare, so why not use it? Deeper meditation can only help you to quiet the relentless mind noise of your ego-driven fears and wants. When you meditate, you hold your power tool in your hands.

"How can I be sure that what I'm doing is enough for me to make constant, conscious contact?"

What you are doing must be working to some degree, Keith, because we are having this conversation, are we not?

"I'm proud to say we are. But I wish I could hear You all the time as clearly as I do now."

Well then, you must continue to work to remove whatever fear is keeping that from happening. When you succeed at that, then you will find your way Home.

"That's wonderful to know, but what about those who think they're guaranteed a place in Heaven just because they think they've been good?"

No matter how "good" someone may be, I guarantee no guarantees if they are only being good because they fear the consequences. Fear is fear. A horse by any other name is still a horse. The only way one can ever become conscious of Absolute Love is by doing the "right" thing because they *want to* out of Love, not because they *have to* out of fear.

"I think I've heard this from You before, but I didn't really understand it until now. You're saying that the only difference between You and me is my fear."

That is exactly what I am saying—a horse is a horse. But before you can harness *your* true horsepower, you must round up all the fears that have kept you from becoming stable—that have kept you from realizing that Love is Love.

"Which fears should I address first, the ones on the surface or my deepest ones?"

Do not risk overloading yourself, Beloved. But if you feel that you can tackle your deepest one now, then go for it, because it is your root fear that first filters the Soul's light.

Many of you move upward in consciousness until you hit a belief barrier that keeps you from the next level. There you remain, grounded in how you think things are, until you can get yourself unstuck from your limiting beliefs, until you can see through the illusion of your fear.

Another major hurdle you must jump is your belief about Satan. For many of you, just the mention of that name brings up a paralyzing, short-winded fear. But I am here to tell you that *that* devil is no more real than Santa! Just read on.

Both Satan (the father of lies) and Santa (fathered by commerce) are nothing but folklore. Tales of the devil have gripped people in a soul-clutch so tight that they prefer to die believing he exists rather than release him back into the nothingness from whence the idea of such a one came. When held up against the Truth of God, any devil is sure to lose! Whose side are you on?

"That goes without saying, but I'll say it anyway — Truth's!"

As for Santa, if you ask a child, "Is Santa real?" he/she says, "Yes!" even though he is not. Unlike children, you know the truth, but your knowing does not negate a child's reality, does it?

"No, not at all. But many may feel that what's being said here is not true."

Yes, I know — another belief. Follow Me on this.

By the time people reach adulthood, they know that the Santa story is fiction. Likewise, based on their own experience, the spiritually mature, no matter their age, know better than to believe the story of Satan. But those who are spiritually still in their youth are not yet far enough along to see through and reject it.

You might find it intriguing to see what happens when you scramble the letters in the word Santa.

"Oh, wow! It says Satan! I never noticed that before."

Yes, it does, My Friend, and it also makes a point.

People believe that Satan, through his temptings, distracts them from God within. The same holds true for Santa. Because their kids believe so strongly in Santa, many adults have become distracted from the true meaning of Christmas (Christ mass)—the time to celebrate the birth of Christ within you. Many have forgotten that Christmas is not a time to receive gifts, but a time to celebrate your own gift. Nor is it the time to convince someone that they must give a gift, but to help them realize that they *are* the gift. Dearest, what I am saying is: what everyone should really want for Christmas is presence.

"I will definitely present this idea to others." (giggling)

As I am doing presently with you? (laughing)

"You know, I just don't get it."

Get what?

"Why some people can't seem to let go of the devil. Is it because they need such a deterrent to keep them from behaving badly?"

Yes, they may be under the assumption that their "let go" behaviors will land them in a fiery pit. But you know what people say about the word 'ass/u/me'? Well, this is just another asinine belief conjured up by those who are Luciferian influenced.

"Since there is no devil, is it more correct to see those who negatively influence us as a lower vibrational force?"

Yes, that is a more accurate depiction.

"Who are the ones being influenced?"

Those most likely to become candidates for manipulation on a psychic level are the ones who are filled with angry, fearful thoughts.

"How can one recognize those who fell under the influence, as You say?"

They are the ones who still promulgate the message that God is separate from you—holier than thou—and that you can never aspire to God because you are born sinners. As if it is a sin to be born human!

"I used to think this way."

How do you feel now that you have relinquished this distorted belief?

"So relieved — much lighter, freer, like a huge burden has been lifted from me, because I know what I was taught is completely untrue."

Just be aware, because there are still influential ones on Earth trying to pump you full of meaningless stuff, all the while keeping secrets from you.

"It appears to me that evil isn't something You look upon kindly."

Appearances can be deceiving, Beloved. Many may not accept this, but I look upon evil with the same compassion as I do everything else. Remember, all I do and all I am is Love!

Absolute

Perfect. Complete; whole. Not mixed; pure.

Not limited. Positive; certain. Actual; real: as an Absolute Truth. Without reference to anything else. That which is thought of as existing in and by itself, without relation to anything else.

Let us look at a belief that many still hold.

I am God	You are Human	The Devil
777 St. Peter St.	1234 Confused Ln.	666 Brimstone Rd.
Cloud 9, Heaven	Anytown, Earth	Center of Earth, Hell
77777	12345	66666

"Yep, that's how most people, especially in the west, think things are — that they are sandwiched between God and the devil." (thinking this doesn't apply to him)

But this is only true to those who make it so by choice. The Absolute Truth is that the Soul is all that exists.

Look back to the definition of fear at the beginning of this chapter. It speaks of reverence or revering. Many do not realize that fearing a devil is actually a form of worship and that when you fear a devil, you surrender to a power other than the Divinity within you.

When a devil appeared before Jesus and offered Him a kingdom of worldly riches, Jesus knew to refuse it because He knew where His Absolute Power came from — God within.

Let me ask you, Keith, if you want to go to the market, do you get there by driving in the opposite direction from where your sustenance awaits?

"No, why would I do that?"

Exactly. You get there by taking the shortest route. If God is your destination, (if you do not want to spiritually starve), you must take the shortest route to Me — the Highway to Heaven — because taking the Highway to Hell can never lead you to My Marketplace!

"What makes it so tough for people to stay on that Highway One?"

Their attitude.

"What do You mean?"

Many choose to live with the "Damned if I do, damned if I don't, so why should I bother with God?" attitude.

"Aren't they cutting off their noses to spite their faces?"

Yes, but I can understand why they might do that. Let Me ask you, how close would *you* want to get to anyone you think is planning to throw you into a pit of fire?

"Not too close! In fact, no distance is far enough away!"

Then this is the time for Me to ask you a few more questions.

"Okay, like what?"

What fears are present in your life?

"I have some small ones, but none that really consume me anymore."

Are you afraid of people?

"No. I love people."

Are you afraid of being afraid?

"You mean do I have anxiety? No, I just don't like being afraid."

You *still* have a fear of Me, right?

"Yes."

Are you afraid of a devil?

"No, *I'm* completely over *that* illusion!"

I beg to differ, Beloved. (calling him on excluding himself earlier)

243

"Really?"

You still have a phantom energy lingering within your subconscious mind, Keith. You get validation of that every time negative entities appear in your dreams. If you were void of this fear, you would not have to ward your demons off as you do.

But you should know that your devil fear is synonymous with your God fear, because, deep down, you still think that if I judge you as "bad," you will land in hell and be tormented.

"Oh my God!"

What is it, my friend?

"I never woulda thought..."

What? (smiling, already knowing the answer)

"I just understood what You've been trying to tell me! I'm the common denominator."

Atta boy!

"I honestly thought that this fear wasn't part of my process anymore. But now that I've gotten how everything in both my waking and my dream world is a reflection of me, I have to ask You — when I finally clear this up, will anyone who comes in contact with me be void of this fear because I am?"

Something like that. When someone who still believes the way you used to believe enters your energy field, your new conviction will work on them at a level they may not be aware of. Nonetheless, it will have the powerful effect of triggering within them the same changes you have found so beneficial.

"So am I to understand that, no matter what we think, no

one can ever be in trouble with You because of our misdeeds?"

Of course not. What purpose would that serve? My existence is not threatened at all by your "bad" choices, so I have no need to make you suffer or do away with you. I much prefer to re-cycle, then nothing I have created is wasted.

"You know, I've never understood the concept that I was born to make mistakes and had to suffer just because I'm human."

If I am Love and I love you, why in the world would I create anything that does not bring Me joy? I ask you the same thing: If there were nothing *you* had to do, why would you create something only to dispose of it?

"Just like You, I wouldn't bother. And I think the reason I'm doing what I love now (at least most of the time) is because I've realized there's nothing I *have* to do, just like You said."

So you are taking on My characteristics, are you?

"Well, yes, I guess I am."

Is living in Love and doing what you love working for you?

"Yes, absolutely!"

So what is it that is still troubling you, My Child? Please do not tell Me it is that whole God and devil thing.

"I know it's some kind of fear, but of what, I don't know."

Would you like some help?

"Sure."

What you are afraid of, Dear One, is power. And it is no wonder, because, from early on, when you did something "wrong," you were reprimanded by those in positions of authority—parents, school principals, the church, law enforcement, etc.

But the Power within you that so much wants to surface is very different from that sort of power. It never punishes. That is because It comes from Me and, unlike those others, I am unconditional. I support you in all the good that you are doing and I shall never punish you for doing whatever you may think of as "bad."

That being said, what do you think happens to someone when they pass to the "other side" with this "sinful" mindset? Do you think one automatically goes to a heavenly realm because I have told you that hell does not exist?

"Hmmm . . ."

Since you still seem a bit perplexed, I shall tell you. Where they go depends entirely on their willingness to let go of the guilt they did not release in life, because if they do not do that, then, when they die, they could end up in the lower astral plane where they will get plenty of the punishment they feel they deserve.

"So are You saying that hell is the lower astral plane?"

Hell is your life gone wrong no matter where you are! But the hell we were just speaking of is the collective consciousness that believes in guilt, punishment, fear—devil.

"Can anyone ever get out of their own hell once they get into it, and do they need Your forgiveness to do so?"

My forgiveness is a given, Beloved. It is up to them to forgive themselves.

"What happens when they do?"

They are reborn.

"You mean redeemed or do You mean reincarnated?"

Both. But whichever next step they take, they are much more apt to live with the forgiveness that will put them closer to choosing Heaven over hell, Life over death, Light over dark, and Love over fear.

"When I was transcribing that last stuff about fear, it triggered something in me."

Share it if you like.

"Years ago, I had horrible thoughts about the world ending in a nuclear holocaust. Sometimes, when it got real bad, my body let me know it. The skin on my hands flaked off, my hair fell out and my teeth began to loosen. Several times, my heart palpitated so much that my girlfriend had to rush me to the emergency room because I thought I was dying of a heart attack!"

All that just from thinking. That kind of anxiety must really be hell!

"Phew, I'm sure glad I got through it! I mean, thinking all those negative thoughts."

That is not entirely accurate, Keith. You still occasionally entertain such thoughts. That is when you put your neck—indeed your whole self—back in that same ol' noose.

"Yeah, that's not 'noose' to me." (giggling)

I guess that is your attempt at gallows humor... (chuckling lightly)

"Please don't get hung up on it!" (guffawing)

I am simply pointing out how you can sometimes be

your own worst enemy. How do you feel now that you have admitted to your past self-abuse?

"Better, somehow reborn, like You said, because I know You will not judge me, no matter what I do."

You are so getting the hang of this! (getting the last laugh) Next question?

"Can a Soul be destroyed?"

Since there is only one Soul—Me—and since everyone is a part of It, if one goes, we all go. And since I am forever, how can any part of Me ever be destroyed?

"Well, how come when I look out into the world, I can see a lot of things being destroyed?"

You may call what you are seeing destruction, but I see it as change. When *you* come from Love instead of fear, you too will be able to see the same restoration and newness in every moment, because coming from Love lets you see everything as something that can be built upon.

Love is perception with no judgment. Love gives you the passion to quietly observe, rebuild, create; to expand instead of destroy. Since all things can and do rehabilitate, you really have no choice but to one day come Home. And, Beloved, one day you shall.

"Thank You for recognizing and reassuring me!"

You have done great Self-work, Keith! You have succeeded in eliminating a lot of your surface issues and some deep-rooted ones as well. So do not be afraid to welcome true power into your life.

*The more you practice
controlling your need
to control,
the more proficient
you will become at it
and the more you will
see every illusion
for what it is —
a golden opportunity.*

RELEASING CONTROL AND LETTING GO

The idea of releasing control will remain an intimidating one as long as you believe that you will experience fear, pain and conflict when you try. But you must learn that letting go is the prerequisite to inviting the peace you truly desire and deserve into your life.

———◆·———

Throw a stone into a still pond and notice how the ripples it creates the moment it hits the surface always spread out to the edge of the pond and then return to the center from whence they originated. The pond's water represents the Universal Mind; the stone is your desire. All the intentions (clear or not) that you have ever tossed into the Cosmic Sea will come back to you in the same way those ripples do.

If you are of clear mind when you throw that first stone

(your intent), you know there is no need for a second one; you know that every pebble of doubt thereafter would only negate the manifesting power of that first toss.

For whatever reason, Dear One, you still do not trust your pitching arm, so you keep on tossing, tossing, tossing to get what you desire. All those ripples look like tidal waves to Me, Keith, like you are wanting, wanting, wanting too much. My hope is that one day soon you will realize that one small stone of intent is all it takes to manifest your life.

"I'm a rock slinger, that's for sure!"

This I know, thus the analogy for you and all to think about.

Do you remember the last chapter wherein I shared with you that the very thing you are afraid of you create by the fears you exhibit at any given moment?

"Yes, I do remember that."

Control falls into this category. So, even though I know you are now easing up on your need to control whenever you can, I suggest you look closer at all you hold dear. The things and concepts that you are clinging to are just your smaller self (ego) seeking what it thinks it needs for happiness.

Perhaps you still think your joy rests with others. Are all your relationships the way you wish them to be?

"Sometimes they are and sometimes they aren't."

When they are not, you must dive even deeper. There is no need to give your power away, or to burden anyone else by putting your fears and blame on their shoulders.

Just share your feelings — that is enough.

"But I get so darned frustrated!"

Yes, I know. I have seen you rise to your boiling point many times. Let me ask you, Dearest, how do you feel from the beginning to the end of your anger?

"Like I must try to take control of the situation and make it go away. But most of the time, I try my best not to act on what I'm feeling, so I just sit there with it."

And how is that working for you?

"Evidently not so hot, because I still run into the same situation a lot."

Do you not see how every time this happens, it means that you are mired in one of your illusions, and how every one of those illusions is also an opportunity?

"Yes, I do. But how do I move out of the illusion and into the opportunity?"

You already know the answer, Keith. You do that by doing what...?

"By letting go of it?"

Ah, yes, Grasshopper! So I suggest that the next time you feel that overwhelming need to control, attempt to control yourself instead.

"Letting go through control — that sounds contradictory."

Yes, but it works.

"It just feels so weird whenever I try."

You may feel panicky at first, but not for long, I assure you, because once you get used to this inverted dynamic, you will begin to notice your resistance disappearing.

Beloved, I also assure you that the more you practice

controlling your need to control, the more proficient you will become at it. And the more you practice, the more you will see how much more you are able to get out of *losing* control than what you were trying to get *through* control. And the benefits will be so much more to your liking.

"That's what happened to me once when I was coming out of my first marriage and I felt like my control was being put to the test."

Yes, you sure took the opportunity to release your hold on that crisis.

"As You say, I turned the whole thing over to my Higher Self. The instant I did that, everything changed for the better. When I woke up the next morning I felt no pain, no fear, no depression — the complete opposite of the torture I endured when my previous relationship broke up."

Bingo! You saw how well letting go can work. Not only do you know there is always another option you *can* choose, but now you know *how* to choose it. But I want you to know that any result you think you may have achieved in that breakup was not a permanent one. Until you get to the bottom of your inner conflicts, whether you are in another partnership or alone, you will continue to wrestle with controlling control.

"What should I do if it comes up again?"

If you find yourself in a situation where there does not seem to be any compromise or common ground, you can exit as you have done before. Without a doubt, to stay where you are not happy reveals that you still crave control. I say do yourself and whoever a favor—just leave!

"But what about religion's views on divorce?"

What about it? I know exactly what religion says about divorce. But you must know that I would rather you be with someone compatible.

"I would think so."

What is the sense of staying in a toxic, strife-filled relationship just because you were taught (and bought) My supposed views about divorce? How could that serve Me and all involved?

"I guess it wouldn't."

So what you do is let go and let God! If compatible companionship is what you truly desire, live that intention and someone will come to you. Remember, just because there is something about someone else that bothers you, you cannot try to change them just to suit yourself.

———◆———

I shall now speak of control on a larger scale. I ask you to write exactly what you are receiving without attachment. I know it will be a challenge because you still think you need to control what is being said. But I see this as an excellent opportunity for you to practice more control relinquishment.

Moses was born into a Hebrew family when Egypt was under the strong arm of Pharaoh. When he was an infant, Moses' mother placed him in a small basket beside the River Nile. She did this to shield him from the soldiers who had been sent by Pharaoh to kill every male child of the Hebrews. She protected her child in the only way she knew how, then hoped against hope that he would survive his ordeal at the river's side.

In a manner of speaking, her prayers were answered because, after a time, Pharaoh's daughter discovered the baby boy's basket nestled amongst the reeds. She felt so much compassion for the infant that she brought him to live in the royal house. As he grew, Moses' daily life was filled with the privileges that only the royals enjoyed. He became every part an Egyptian, except for the blood that coursed through his veins.

"I don't understand why so many children were killed and why only the males?"

So that the Egyptians would never have to face a rebellion led by Hebrew men. Little did they know that what they were about to be confronted with would be far more daunting and beyond their ability to control.

There came a time when Moses killed an Egyptian for striking a Hebrew, and then he buried him in the sand. When Pharaoh found out about what Moses had done, he banished him to the desert.

While wandering in search of physical and spiritual sustenance, Moses learned of his lineage and began to turn his attention to his true people, the Hebrews. His compassion for his tribe led him to Me for the guidance he needed to free them. It was then that I focused My attention on him and it was then that Moses became True Royalty, not in the house of Pharaoh, but in the House of God.

One day, Moses set out to climb Mount Sinai because he believed that something of great spiritual significance was happening at its peak. He had seen a fire in the sky that engulfed it, and he took it as a sign from Me that could not be ignored.

His instincts were soon proven right. There, on the mountaintop, he was instructed to descend, go to Pharaoh and inform him of what would happen if Pharaoh did not let his people go. But when Moses and his brother Aaron brought God's warning to Pharaoh, the ruler chose to ignore him, assuming that his power struggle was only with this one man. How could he know that, within this simple man, the True God was alive!

Pharaoh's overconfidence and failure to act brought on an onslaught of plagues so devastating that life as the Egyptians knew it ceased to be. When Pharaoh had finally had enough, he brought Moses before him one more time and told him to take his people away from Egypt at last.

I have told you this Bible story to illustrate how people who want to rule the world can never have enough control.

Today, if absolute power were to fall into the hands of a dictator such as Hitler, Mussolini, Franco, Stalin or Mao Tse Tung, over time, it would lead to world, galactic and cosmic upheaval. Because your technology is so sophisticated, their control would spread like a deadly virus and freedom throughout the universe would perish.

Moses was a messenger, a Son of God, who led the people of Israel to liberation. The same message is now being brought through you, another instrument of Mine, to remind and assure everyone that they need no longer be controlled by fear, that they will soon be released from their spiritual bondage.

Here is the interplay of Moses and Pharaoh straight from the Bible. It is offered to show you how Divine cleansing will take place yet again. Exactly how is it going to happen? That will be up to all of you!

Excerpts from Exodus 6, 10 and 11

6 So Jehovah said to Moses: "Now you will see what I shall do to Pharaoh, because on account of a strong hand he will send them away and on account of a strong hand he will drive them out of his land."

2 And God went on to speak to Moses and say to him: "I am Jehovah. 3 And I used to appear to Abraham, Isaac and Jacob as God Almighty, but as respects My Name Jehovah I did not make My Self known to them. 4 And I also established my covenant with them to give the land of Ca'naan, the land of their alien residences in which they reside as aliens. 5 And I, even I, have heard the groaning of the sons of Israel, whom the Egyptians are enslaving, and I remember my covenant.

6 Therefore say to the sons of Israel, I am Jehovah, and I shall certainly bring you out from under the burdens of the Egyptians and deliver you from their slavery, and I shall indeed

reclaim you with an outstretched arm and with great judgments. [7] And I shall certainly take you to me as a people, and I shall indeed prove to be God to you; and you will certainly know that I am Jehovah your God who is bringing you out of the burdens of Egypt. [8] And I shall certainly bring you into the land that I raised my hand in oath to give to Abraham, Isaac and Jacob; and I shall indeed give it to you as something to possess. I am Jehovah."

[9] Afterward Moses spoke to this effect to the sons of Israel, but they did not listen to Moses out of discouragement and for the hard slavery.

10 Then Jehovah said to Moses: "Go in to Pharaoh, because I have let his heart and the hearts of his servants become unresponsive, in order that I may set up these signs of mine right before him, [2] and in order that you may declare in the ears of your son and your son's son how severely I have dealt with Egypt and my signs that I have established among them; and you will certainly know that I am Jehovah."

[3] So Moses and Aaron went in to Pharaoh and said to him: "This is what Jehovah the God of the Hebrews has said: 'How long must you refuse to submit yourself to me? Send my people away that they may serve me. [4] For if you continue refusing to send my people away, here

I am bringing locusts within your boundaries tomorrow. 5 And they will actually cover the visible surface of the earth and it will not be possible to see the earth; and they will simply eat up the rest of what has escaped, what has been left to you people by the hail, and they will certainly eat every sprouting tree of yours out of the field. 6 And your houses and the houses of all your servants and the houses of all Egypt will be filled to an extent that your fathers and your fathers' fathers have not seen it from the day of their existing upon the ground until this day." With that he turned and went out from Pharaoh.

27 At this Jehovah let Pharaoh's heart become obstinate, and he did not consent to send them away. 28 So Pharaoh said to him: "Get out from me! Watch yourself! Do not try to see my face again, because on the day of your seeing my face you will die." 29 To this Moses said: "That is the way you have spoken. I shall not try to see your face anymore."

11 And Jehovah proceeded to say to Moses: "One more plague I am going to bring upon the Pharaoh and Egypt. After that he will send you away from here. At the time he sends you away altogether, he will literally drive you out from here. 2 Speak, now, in the ears of the people,

that they should ask every man of his companion and every woman of her companion articles of silver and articles of gold." 3 Accordingly Jehovah gave the people favor in the eyes of the Egyptians. The man Moses too was very great in the land of Egypt, in the eyes of Pharaoh's servants and in the eyes of the people.

4 And Moses went on to say: "This is what Jehovah has said, 'About midnight I am going out into the midst of Egypt, 5 and every firstborn in the land of Egypt must die, from the firstborn of Pharaoh who is sitting on his throne to the firstborn of the maidservant who is at the hand mill and every firstborn of beast. 6 And there will certainly occur a great outcry in all the land of Egypt, the like of which has never yet occurred, and the like of which will never be brought about again. 7 But against any of the sons of Israel will no dog move eagerly its tongue, from man to beast; in order that you people may know Jehovah can make a distinction between the Egyptians and the sons of Israel.' 8 And all these servants of yours will certainly come down to me and prostrate themselves to me, saying, 'Go, all of you the people who follow your steps.' And after that I shall go out." With that he went out from Pharaoh in the heat of anger.

9 Then Jehovah said to Moses: "Pharaoh will

not listen to you men, in order for my miracles to be increased in the land of Egypt." [10] And Moses and Aaron performed all these miracles before Pharaoh; but Jehovah would let Pharaoh's heart become obstinate, so that he did not send the sons of Israel away from his land.

———————◆———————

"When will this cleansing occur?

It is happening now, Keith. Take a look around. Can you not see how the infrastructures of family, religion, education and geopolitics are all beginning to weaken?

"Without a doubt. But I also see a lot of people who want to build, and are building, their lives on truth. I see it on Oprah, the news — heck, I can see it in the eyes of people who don't even know they're searching. It seems like almost everyone is looking for something to fill the hole we all feel inside. What's going on?"

I am answering people's prayers!

"Huh?"

You seem to think that the rebuilding of society and everyone's search for truth are different from one another, but they are one and the same. You are all creating these changes by finally recognizing the illusion you have been living in, by realizing your relationship to a cause greater than yourselves, and by deciding to take that cause up. It is through this new perception that you are becoming more globally aware, watching everything that takes place within the institutions at work in your modern world. Now, when mishaps happen, you demand answers.

"Will we ever know all the answers, I mean the truth about all the things that have been kept from us?"

If you continue your quest for Me, indeed you will, because all questions will fall by the wayside when I become your Answer—the Answer within, the Answer without question!

What I am saying is that once everyone begins to establish the Divine within themselves, you will find the solution to all of your problems. You are on the cusp of choosing your fate.

"What is it that we need to do to ensure that we make it?"

Take responsibility for everything that happens and tolerate nothing that is not in alignment with where you want to be.

"I'm sure that giving up our desire to acquire stuff wouldn't hurt either."

No, it would not. But surrender does not only require you to release your want for possessions; it also means you must abandon the dogmatic religious, cultural and political beliefs instilled in you by those who want to control. You must back out of those systems completely if you are not being fed loving spoonfuls of universal truth.

"I've met many who walk the path of universal truth, but are there enough of us to cause the world to shift?"

All over the world there are men and women who are living such exemplary lives that they elevate the consciousness of their entire sphere of acquaintances. There are enough of you, all right. It is *when* you will make the shift that remains in question. Pray that it will not take too long, because a few years hence, Christ the Good Shepherd will be ready to gather His flock.

———————•◆•———————

As you may have noticed, many things are also going on in the political arena. True leaders are rising and making changes, while deceitful leaders are falling fast and hard.

"What are Your thoughts about our voting process?"

Understand that if someone in power leads by using manipulation and untruths, he/she is treading on thin ice. When you vote for that leader, you are skating on the same thin ice.

I am aware that you have blindly elected some into office, only to be shocked at what they have done (or not done) after their seat of power became a comfortable one. This is why I continue to expose your leaders' ill-advised agendas, so that you can get the "bad ones" out and thus avoid the karma you would be destined for if they remained in power.

Know that I do support the notion of leadership, but from what I have seen thus far, the track records of many of those whom you have elected have been "poor." Yes, there have been moments in history when true leaders have appeared, but just as they were on their way to making positive changes, they were assassinated, leaving their visions to die on the vine.

My question to all of you is: Will you continue to follow leaders who care only about themselves, or will you accept Leadership from the One who cares only about the welfare of humanity?

"Please tell me how we can make this happen."

First, do not allow what has been taking place to continue! It is your Divine birthright to rise up against any leadership if it does not set you on course towards a transcended consciousness. This may sound like I am supporting rebellion, but that is not entirely true, because I do not support upheaval and anarchy. But I *do* support your doing whatever it takes to uproot any and all weeds that could stifle the potential of your Eden!

Second, when you seek leaders, make certain they have a Divine calling, and are not someone you vote for just because they seem to be the "best" ones running. Unlike the leaders of the present system, Divine leaders will not even hint to you that they are the ones in charge. They will govern righteously and be of service to you all.

Third, make certain your chosen leaders have a direct connection to the Divine so that, in any situation, they can move to the good by praying to God, "What do I do?"

If you are not choosing leaders with these qualifications, why do you even bother to vote?

"To try to make some kind of difference."

Psssst...I will let you in on a little secret. Sometimes your votes are not even a factor. Many will try to convince you that the election process is a legitimate one. But do not be fooled. Election results are often determined long before you step into the voting booth. Some may dispute this, but there is no point. What do you think happened in your 2000 presidential election?

"I'm not really sure."

That unwieldy political fiasco came to light when the Divine intervened and exposed it.

"So why are we even allowed to vote if one candidate is going to win regardless of who we choose?"

Those in the system want you to keep believing you have a say in the matter. In 2000, they used the ploy of a ballot foul-up to convince you that you count. But even though the election mess provided both an excuse and a diversion, it did not dull citizen awareness, because people were able to clearly see that something was amiss.

"Since so many of us will be paying closer attention to the voting process from now on, it'll probably be much harder for anyone to make such questionable moves. If they try, they'll be stopped and that'll open the door for a Divine leader to walk through."

Keep in mind what I said earlier—your present legislative branch will collapse, and it will take years to rebuild it. Because of this restoration process, many old guard politicians will be forced out. Your new lawmakers will not make law, *per se*, but rather, will introduce you to Divine Law and teach you how to fall into flow with It. Remember, too, that the establishment of Divine Order is commencing as I speak!

That said, it will not do anyone any good to be angry or judgmental about what has happened or even what may happen. Do not harden your hearts to the point that you do not trust any worthy ones who may enter the political arena. If you look to any of them with the intention of finding fault, that will be your own fault. On the other hand, if you forgive both them and yourselves for whatever you perceive as your shortcomings, you will see that it is My intervention that enabled you to select and accept new leadership and guidance.

"So what can we do to speed things up even more?"

Change your logic. Most believe if they vote for the least "bad" one, that will keep the "worst" one out. This reasoning will not work because, even if you vote for the "better," or shall I say, the one not as "bad," you are still helping a controlling system to stay alive.

Here is what you can do: you can simply choose not to vote unless and until there are worthy candidates to vote for. You need not buy into a bad system that depends on you to stay afloat.

"And if no one votes?"

Someone will step up anyway to be the mouthpiece for power.

"How many people are actually 'in control' and what is it they really want?"

There are only a few and what they want most is what no one else has.

"What would that be?"

Something beyond the money, oil, property or power they already have. What they want is galactic power.

Keith, I know you have seen the first *Indiana Jones* movie, and I am here to tell you that its story is not that far removed from what is taking place now.

"Really? How so?"

As the movie depicts, the quest for power reaches far beyond Earth, and there are those few who will stop at nothing to get their hands on it. So, to keep such a thing from happening (as it did in the movie), the Spirit of God is constantly moving in cycles and staying ever vigilant.

Again I question, why do you put so much faith and energy into a system that binds you?

"I don't know what to say except that's what's always been done. Besides, there are many who say that we still have a pretty good government."

You are missing the point, Keith. Why do you need someone else to control you? Can you not control yourselves?

"I see what You mean."

There are many who say they love their government and country, even though they harbor past-life memories of those they love being persecuted by one power establishment or another. They may not realize it yet, but deep in their hearts they too desire a dramatic change.

Yes, in times past, power junkies engaged in all sorts of atrocities. They succeeded in putting an end to nations, exterminating races of people and murdering countless individuals. They crucified Jesus, assassinated Abraham Lincoln, John and Robert Kennedy, Martin Luther King, and stomped out the fire of many others who were trying to build a better world.

Do the research and confirm for yourself what it is that

the few in power are still seeking, that, if found, will enable them to govern the destiny of the whole world. When you do, I hope you are sitting down, because what will be revealed may knock you for a loop!

"Sounds very interesting."

So it is, My Friend. And if and when you source this out, I will lead you to the knowledge that best serves you.

As I said before, not everyone in positions of power wants more or cares about the struggle for it. Any member of the clergy or any political person who operates from a selfless heart serves Me sincerely.

My Children: I know that you believe in God. But if you want to help Me help you shape the world into something worth living in, it is not enough to simply believe in Me — you must know Me as I know you. And know that I am ready to do what I have always done — work through ordinary people just like you who are making themselves available to anchor the Divine Principle.

Ignorance invites fear.
The most powerful tool
to eliminate fear
is a mind open
to receiving information.

This is why I come:
to enlighten everyone
so that you will not be
left trembling in the dark.

THE RETURN OF CHRIST

"Some believe that Jesus will arrive on a white horse; that His coming will be signaled by the parting of clouds, heralded by the trumpeting of angels. Others believe that Christ will be manifested only in the souls who make themselves available. Which is correct?"

Here is the most accurate way to view the return of Christ: it is not an either/or situation. It would be more correct to say that both these scenarios are facets of the truth.

———◆·———

Yes, the white horse is true, but not in the way many imagine. That prophecy refers to the comet Hale-Bopp that hurtled through space in the 98th year of the last century. The purpose of its trajectory was to give the world an advance sign of the return of the One you have known as Jesus.

"When will He return?"

Would you believe Me if I told you that He is already on Earth?

"Right now?"

Yes, He arrived as a child in July of 2000. The white-tailed comet was the metaphorical horse upon which He arrived.

"You mean . . ."

Yes, Keith, I mean that the dream experience you had eighteen years ago *was* real—Jesus has been born again as one of you. Time and again over the past few years, I have offered you validation of this, especially when you were in India. Why is the truth so difficult for you to believe and accept?

"I don't think I can answer Your question right now."

Because of what you think others might say about you when this book enters the public's field of awareness?

"Yes, I'm sure that's a major part of it."

I recognize your reservations, but if you have concerns about people's "How dare you!" attitude, then the best way to respond to them is with understanding and love.

"It doesn't seem to matter how many times You tell me, I still worry that this 'Jesus is born again' idea is something I've concocted in my head. Surely You can see how nervous I am about this."

What is it you are trying to say?

"I want to do the 'right' thing!"

Yes, I know, and your intention to do just that is why I am telling you this.

"Please tell me again exactly what You would like me to do?"

Your job is to inform others about Jesus' return as a person. I admit, it will not be an easy task because, as we just spoke of, many have expectations that He will show up in one particular way or another.

"Will You tell me where He was born this time?"

Patience, Dear One. I shall not be revealing that to you just yet. Right now, it is enough for you to know that His human presence will be integral to Divine energies becoming more firmly anchored.

"Why is He hidden from the public's awareness?"

There are two reasons. The first is so that He can avoid distractions and unwanted attention as He prepares for His actual appearance.

The second is because He is not yet ready, nor are you. If He goes public too soon, many will not believe their eyes nor take well to the idea that He has come. Until there has been enough of a shift in clarity and understanding, His entrance will serve no purpose.

You see, there is an order to the Divine Will that must play out in sequence. At the right time, He will set out to help humanity transcend its collective ego by showing you the difference between reality (living in Love) and non-reality (living in fear). Thus will the pandemic of fear and greed come to an end.

As for Christ manifesting in individuals, well, right now, there are many such active souls on Earth, yourself included. Some of you will not only pave the way for the

Teacher whose sole/Soul purpose is to give of Himself as He did before, but you will also deflect any who would try to thwart His mission.

"What do You mean? He *is* Jesus the Christ, so doesn't He have enough power to protect Himself from any adversaries?"

Oh, you mean the same power He had the last time—when He was crucified?

"I see Your point."

As I said, you each have your part to play.

"God, I pray that I can be in His inner circle, be there with Him and for Him to help in any way I can!"

Beloved, you are already in His inner circle and you are being a great help by writing the words you are writing about Him. But He is not done with you yet.

"What do You mean?"

A few years hence, He will come to you again and give you instructions about further work you are to do.

"But what..."

I know your mind must be racing, Keith, but for now, just rest it. In time, all your questions will be cleared up.

"Phew! I'll try."

Now that the birth has happened, do not be surprised if you wake up one morning and find that something inside you just feels different. And do not be surprised if the whole world feels the same way, even though their reactions may not be the same as yours. Many will choose to talk about the changes they are feeling; many more will purposely deny and ignore them. But, since you are aligning yourself, you will know intuitively what is soon to transpire.

"And what will that be?"

Jesus announcing His presence in the world.

"Doesn't Scripture state that no one except God in Heaven is supposed to know of His return and that it will come like a thief in the night?"

Yes, it is true that I am the only One who knows, but now I am telling you. And even though people will learn this from your work, when He does show up, you can bet that some will still cry "false prophet" or say that Satan has disguised himself as the Holy Light mentioned in Scripture (2 Corinthians 11:13–15). You can bet the news of His coming will spark much debate.

What the other part of the passage means is that if one does not develop the Christ within themselves — because they are too busy looking outward and/or skyward — then Christ will pass them by like a thief in the night. The only way for anyone to truly believe that He is who He says He is, is to develop the ability to recognize Truth within themselves.

I will tell you how to recognize not only Jesus, but any true teacher of God:

1) If the teacher teaches unconditional love.

2) If the teacher does not claim to be god over you, but rather, helps you to see that you are his/her equal in God.

275

Dear One, you have mentioned several times how concerned you are with what you are receiving and writing. Let Me assure you that the Source is a Pure One. My concern is about what you will do with it. Will you close this manuscript now, never to write in it again, or do you want to continue?

"I'm really loving what I'm learning. Keep it coming!"

Good, because I have more to share with you.

Jesus, like you, was born to natural parents. The purpose of His return to Earth as a human is so that you can all see the Christ Light in yourselves once again. And as you come to see His humanity, you will also see your own divinity.

"Will He begin to teach as a child or will He wait until He is older?"

He will begin very early by exemplifying the childlike qualities of purity, innocence, acceptance and wonderment. His simple ways will serve as a counterpoint to the arrogance of adults and show them how, by living their lives the way they have, their egos have been allowed to take root, grow and bring about the chaos of today's world.

Yes, Jesus will begin to actively teach those around Him, sharing His genuine, pure disposition for all to see (the same as every child's before he/she is tainted with dogma, rules and ideas of separation).

When He makes Himself known, many will be afraid. But let Me make it clear that it is not the Child they will fear. What will cause them to be afraid will be their refusal to let go of their long-held beliefs.

Insofar as enlightenment is concerned, ignorance is not

bliss. All ignorance does is invite fear. The most powerful tool to eliminate fear is a mind open to receiving information. This is why I come: to enlighten everyone so that you will not be left trembling in the dark.

Let Me expound further on the other Christs that are active now. They are everywhere imaginable! One could be living next door to you; one could be standing behind you in the checkout line; one could be your newspaper boy or your bank teller. All, like you, are committed to becoming conscious. They are working on themselves to prepare for change, all the while promulgating the changes they are on Earth to bring about. They see themselves as the crew of the Messiah-ship, the ones who will lead everyone to the Mother-ship.

Some of these Christ apprentices—the Children of Light—are born with special abilities and can do things beyond what some may be willing to believe or accept. Some are living amongst you and more will come, bringing with them Divine Vision and Divine Power.

For example, there are children living in South America who display phenomenal feats of telekinesis, who can bend spoons and move objects without touching them. If you ever come in contact with any of these children, look into their eyes and you will see the Light of Spirit.

These children (who are beginning to gather together) are different from most, for they are born with an intact awareness. They know where they have been, they know who they are and they know the purpose of their mission.

Furthermore, unlike most adults who have only two

active DNA strands, these children have between eight and twelve active strands of DNA. It is in these multiple active strands that the Children of Light store Divine information and power they can use at will. And, since their will is unified with that of the Divine Will, they act accordingly.

"So You're telling me I only have two strands? What's up with that?"

Nothing personal, Keith, just a fail-safe means to keep everyone from abusing everyone else. There are far too many people that would use such power to control, so I only bestow it on those who are conscious of My plan.

"I see what You mean. I can't tell You how many times I hear people say, "Kids nowadays are disturbed, nothing but rebellious out-of-control punks that must be restrained.""

Let Me ask you, does attempting to control them ever work?

"Hardly ever."

How right you are! Even when adults attempt to exercise control, kids still express themselves in the very behaviors that adults are trying to discourage. I give children freedom of expression and adults try to take it away —go figure!

Oh, I agree, kids *are* rebellious and it is in their very nature to oppose anyone who tries to extinguish their spirit's light. The way they dress, many have a problem with. The way they look, many have a problem with. The way they act, many have a problem with. What they think they stand for, many have a problem with. Whatever they do that differs from the norm, many have a problem with.

Indeed, who they are, many have a problem with.

"No wonder they rebel!"

But all these problems really begin with the ones who regard kids' behavior as a problem. You see, it is no big deal to Me if kids get tattoos or pierce every body part. What "concerns" Me is those who would try to pierce children's hearts with the daggers of their own egos!

The intent of every adult should be to never hurt children, but rather to help them reach their fullest potential to inspire change. When you find it within yourselves to be permissive, grateful and humble around them, it will help all of you to acknowledge who you once were and, in essence, still are, and why I bestow power upon the Children of Light and not adults.

Yes, you as adults must acknowledge children as people. Learn what they have to offer you. Sit and talk with them for a while and they will enlighten you with the simple wisdom that can only be coming from deep within.

Children should not be thought of as delinquents! Believe it or not, they have the vision to improve your world—if only you will let them. All they ask is the right of Self-expression. But the truth is, they need not ask. You see, I have already given them *My* permission!

"Earlier, You said that special children are gathering. How many are there?"

Interesting you should ask. They number fewer than you might imagine and they do not behave that differently from the way you did in your adolescence.

The Children of Light prefer to join up with "normal"

kids and run as a pack. That way, they can live amongst you, yet remain hidden from the "wolves" until the time is right.

"So You're saying that the kids they run with have a purpose as well."

Yes, and together they form the mission of the Children of Light.

"Do these Children of Light live only in South America?"

Not necessarily, but no matter where they are, those imbued with Spirit's power are lying low until the time is right. When that time comes, they will emerge and lead the way to change. What do you think people will do then?

"I think many will boycott anything they have to offer."

Right you are. Once again, what they say and do, many will have a problem with! But try to thwart it (though some might), an awareness will happen and eventually people will understand.

"This may be off the subject, but I want to tell You how sad I am that we adults have managed to screw up the world so badly."

Ah, but that *is* indeed the subject, Beloved, and that will change!

"When?"

When you choose to follow the guidance of a special Child. I bet you never thought that a child would be the one to set you on your spiritual path.

"Oh, Jesus, of course! It's all beginning to make sense to me now. Based on what I've learned, it *would* take a child to save us from ourselves!"

Together, these Children will teach Self-expression.
Together, these Children will teach Peace.
Together, these Children will teach Love.
And together, these Children will teach Unity—God.

PREPARE FOR THE RETURN OF THE CHRIST!

When they saw Him,
they all fell to their knees.
He said to them,
'Lift yourself up to Me,
for you are My brothers —
all of you!'

My Revelation

Right now is a good time for you to tell the dream you had so long ago, My Friend.
"I'll give it my best shot."
That is good enough for Me.

Before I begin, I must say to all my readers that I'll try to convey what took place, though what I'm about to share with you is very challenging for me to put into words.

One night, I had an experience that completely blew my mind. It left me no choice but to develop myself spiritually so that I could understand why I'd had this prophetic vision and to grasp its meaning when it came to pass. This is a record of my experience.

———— • ◆ • ————

About eighteen years ago, Jesus appeared to me while I was asleep and asked me to come with Him. With my permission, He released my consciousness from my body and showed me humanity's past, present and future.

> *The Revelation of Jesus Christ, which God gave unto him, to show unto his servants things which must shortly come to pass; and he sent and signified it by his angel unto his servant John. (Revelation 1:1)*

As we began to "fly away," I somehow knew it was the dawn of my new day. Once we got to our destination, I opened my eyes to find myself suspended fifty feet above the ground. Even though the sun had not yet risen, I could clearly see rolling hills stretching out in every direction, all they way to the horizon. Next thing I knew, millions of naked men (but no women) appeared from nowhere to occupy every square inch of this expanse. They were divided into groups of thirty or so by long fences that stood about three feet high.

I sensed Jesus all around me. Along with feeling comforted by His Presence, I was overcome by a feeling of lightness that I knew was both powerful and significant. I knew the Book of Heaven had opened and God would soon cast His "judgment" (Light) upon man to reveal his sins (darkness).

> *And when he had opened the seventh seal, there was silence in heaven about the space of half an hour. (Revelation 8:1)*

I heard the voice of Jesus say to me, "Concentrate now as

you look from east to west." As I did what He said, I saw that the men below were no longer naked. Those in the most easterly groups were now wearing one-piece jumpsuits of the purest white I'd ever seen — so many of them that the line they formed seemed to stretch from north to south unto infinity.

As my eyes continued to pan, I saw that the men standing behind the first row were now wearing white as well, but their suits seemed to be touched by cream. This line, too, seemed to extend from north to south unto infinity.

Looking further west, I saw that the third row of men had jumpsuits that were creamy white also, but now the cream color seemed to be even more dominant. Row after row, this gradation of colors progressed.

Casting my eyes westward, I beheld countless rows of men clad in jumpsuits of every shade of yellow, green, blue, purple, red and black. Then, with one last panoramic sweep, I witnessed the entire spectrum of humanity seamlessly blend together from east to west.

Once again, I heard Jesus' voice, "Keith, look to the east and you will see the risen sun/Son that will bring warmth and light to the world." As I was following His instruction, Jesus actually appeared and stood beside me. I was so humbled that I began to genuflect. Before I could reach the ground, He said, "Lift yourself up to Me, for you are My brother." His words elated me. And then, with a wave of His hand, the Lord materialized a platform for us to stand on so that He could reveal Himself to all the men below.

When they saw Him, they too fell to their knees, so He said to them what He had just said to me, "Lift yourself up to

Me, for you are My brothers — all of you!" Then, as their eyes raised to look upon Him, Jesus spoke His Heart:

"I stand before all of humanity to tell you that the time for change is here — the time for peace and the time to receive your gift of power and freedom!"

> *Blessed is he that readeth, and they that hear the words of this prophecy, and keep those things which are written therein: for the time is at hand. (Revelation 1:3)*

As a sign of their thirst for freedom, the multi-hued human mass responded to His words in perfect unison by beginning to shout a mantra. Calling upon the Absolute God for succor, the men thrust their arms up toward the sky, all the while continuing to chant the mantra "Christ." It was clear to me they were proclaiming, "We are ready!"

> *Behold, he cometh with clouds; and every eye shall see him, and they also which pierced him: and all kindreds of the earth shall wail because of him. Even so, Amen. (Revelation 1:7)*

As I beheld this magnificent spectacle, Jesus turned to me and quietly said, "My brother, *there is no difference between you and Me.* Are you willing to incarnate so that you can tell the world this truth? Are you willing to spread the Word, which is God's Will, to all men?"

> *Who bare record of the word of God, and of the testimony of Jesus Christ, and of all things that he saw. (Revelation 1:2) Write the things which thou*

hast seen, and the things which are, and the things which shall be hereafter. (Revelation 1:19)

I felt so honored that I didn't hesitate for a minute. I agreed to do what my Lord had asked me to do. And at that very moment, for only a moment, I blacked out. When I came to, I was quite dumbfounded to find myself wearing a red jumpsuit, standing amidst the shouting throngs, thrusting my own fist up to Heaven right along with them. I intuitively knew I had become a part of the world I have now come to know.

The Christed One spoke again, repeating, "I address all men! The time has come for change. So let it begin!" As we rousingly acknowledged His words one last time, He vanished. But even though He was gone, I knew that He would surely return to walk among us and become actively involved with the change he had charged us all with helping Him to bring about.

My mind tried to make sense of the ongoing experience I was having. It was then that God the Father interrupted my feeble attempts at logic and spoke into my Soul, "Behold the Holy Spirit!"

I was in the Spirit on the Lord's day, and heard behind me a great voice, as of a trumpet. (Revelation 1:1)

As God spoke, my heart overflowed with serenity. Standing with the other men, I watched in wonder as the Dove of the Holy Spirit, in the form of a delicate mist, descended from the sky and quickly began to drape the men in white. At almost the same time, a cocoon-like pod of light arose from the ground and engulfed their bodies. Then, before my mesmerized eyes, they sank into the earth.

I trembled with anticipation as I watched the mist rapidly advancing towards *my* row. The moment the Holy Spirit descended upon me and moved through me, all the fears I'd ever had disappeared, and I could at long last see my Self as God's Love. I felt the Holy Spirit wrap me in my own finely woven cocoon of light, then I joined the others who had already been absorbed into the earth where we were to remain, dormant, until the return of the Christed One.

At this point, I went through another brief blackout phase. When I awoke from what seemed like long, deep sleep, Jesus was there to greet me. He said, "Keith, we are now inside the earth." Indeed, as I looked around, all the men from my row aboveground were there with Jesus and me in a large cubicle made of earth. Backlit by dim lanterns, the Lord spoke to me once more, saying, "My brother, I was not sure if you were going to make it through the hibernation."

And I turned to see the voice that spake with me. And being turned, I saw seven golden candlesticks. (Revelation 1:12)

I asked the Lord how long we had been there. Jesus replied, "For eighteen years, all the while growing our light bodies for the Coming. We need to go now for there is much work to do! Are you ready?" "Ready for what?" I replied. "The world above us is warring — engaged in its hopeless battle of separation. We Warriors of Light have been called upon to bring about the Divine Intervention." Humbly, I said, "I'm honored to be an instrument for peace!"

Just then, a question entered my mind: "What is the significance of our red suits and why are other groups' uniforms different from ours?" "The difference is a metaphor for separation. It signifies the way humanity has allowed itself to become divided by color, class, religion and geopolitics. But now

I

Am

Here

to transform everyone through this lesson."

Jesus pointed to both of our garments and said, "Your suit is red, correct?" "Yes," I answered.

> *And in the midst of the seven candlesticks one like unto the Son of man, clothed with a garment down to the foot, and girt about the paps with a golden girdle. (Revelation 1:13)*

"In the past, the way you humans have regarded those clothed in different-colored suits has determined how much you have chosen to separate from others. If they had been wearing orange, you would have embraced them, because red is relative to orange. You would have considered them to be your allies." Then Jesus went on to describe how red and yellow create orange.

"You have always considered those wearing yellow jumpsuits to be 'the enemy'." "Why?" I asked, confused. "Because yellow and red have no relationship to one another in the grand illusion."

I suddenly realized that the men in orange could be my allies or my enemies, depending solely on how I chose to regard them. I understood that this same premise would hold true for my relationships with the men clad in blue, yellow and green.

As I slowly began to grasp the meaning of Jesus' words, I was mortified by the images playing out in my mind: enemies could kill their enemies; enemies could kill their allies; allies from all sides could kill each other. The message became painfully clear: we are all going to die!

The Lord then said, "If people could only see the bigger picture, the world would become a mighty planetary power and be able to assist me in spiritually illuminating the solar system. The solar system would then illuminate the galaxy; the galaxy would then illuminate the universe; the universe would then illuminate the omniverse; the omniverse would then illuminate the omniverses.

From planet→solar system, from galactic→cosmic — it all starts with everyone in the world working as one. This is why I have come this time — to unify the Alpha and the Omega!"

I am Alpha and Omega, the beginning and the ending, saith the Lord, which is, and which was, and which is to come, the Almighty. (Revelation 1:8)

Overcome with an immense Love and a sense of duty, I

silently vowed my life to service. Aloud, I said, "We do not have to go through this!" In that moment, I felt the Christ well up inside of me and I was born! I ascended to the earth's surface at once to carry out the agreement I had made with Jesus.

———◆———

Every time I reflect back on that vision I had all those years ago, it makes me long to see Jesus again, but I know I must be patient. In the meantime, I do my best to focus on the good that connects people to people and all of us to God.

Since I have touched the Divine — since I have had the chance to see the Light — I now know that our mundane vision of separation has no bearing whatsoever on the Truth of what is. The Truth is: God is all there is!

Begin to feel.
Begin to touch.
Begin to see.
Begin to listen.
Begin to know.
Begin to be.
Begin!

LOOK WITHIN

How are you feeling today, Keith?

"Pretty good, but there are some pretty intense things going on with me."

Sounds like you are in the perfect space to write one more chapter.

"What shall I write about this time?"

Why not tell more about your own life. Share with our readers how you acquired the awareness that enabled you to write this book. After that, I shall write one final chapter.

"Sounds good to me."

———◆———

For most of my life up until 1992, I was rebellious and lost. I didn't really give a damn about anything. I wanted what I wanted when I wanted it and it didn't really matter how I got it. But after Jennifer and I broke up, I began to change. At the same time I was falling apart, I somehow knew that in order for me to survive, I would have to seek Spirit. It's hard to find the words to explain what it felt like when that finally hit me, but I'll try.

Everything was dark! I was desperately alone, utterly depressed and suffering excruciating heart pangs all the time. Looking back, I don't remember actually deciding to pray, but one day I just found myself doing it, not once, but several times. The next day, same thing, and for every day thereafter. The prayer I remember saying most was, "God, I really need Your help."

One night after my band's rehearsal, the guys were going over to Chris' house. They'd never asked me to join them before because they knew I wasn't really into the "New Age stuff" they were into. But that night, for some reason, I was invited to come along. I said sure, thinking that all we were going to do was just hang out and party. Boy, was I wrong!

No sooner had we sat down in Chris' little upstairs room, than my bandmates and one other friend who'd joined us began to talk about that "weird stuff." I just sat there, drinking my drink, listening to them go at it. But eventually my curiosity was piqued, because the things my friend Mike was saying seemed so relevant to what I was going through.

After a few minutes, I asked if he could interpret a dream I'd had in which Jesus appeared to me and told me the word 'Yam' three times. Mike asked me if there there'd been more to my experience and, if so, would I share it. I said sure.

"It was really weird," I said. "In what way?" he asked. "Jesus seemed to be behind me and up towards the ceiling, but I could see Him perfectly. At the same time, I could feel myself floating up there, too. But I didn't want any part of that, so, I somehow made myself wake up." "Is that it?" Mike asked. "Yep, that's it," I told him. "Guy, that is so cool!" he said. Then he got up and walked over to the bookshelf, selected one book and brought it back to where I was sitting. He opened it to show me the meaning of 'Yam' — the sound of the spiritual heart (the heart chakra), and his gesture touched me to my core. Yes, I knew in my own heart of hearts that something had awakened and there was no turning back.

From that evening on, whenever I was feeling down from obsessing about Jennifer, I called Mike and found much comfort in his words. Not only did he help me see things in a more realistic light, he also seemed to have an uncanny way of getting me to open up so that, for the very first time, I could begin to see my self/Self.

One day he asked me, "Without judging yourself, Keith, tell me, do you like your life?" I said, "Hell no!" His next question was, "What are you willing to do to have peace?" I told him, "At this point, I'm willing to try just about anything!" "Then prepare yourself for miracles," he said.

For the next hour or so, he laid out some principles I could begin to work with. But at the same time, he suggested I not believe a word he was saying! He said, "Just let the manifestations speak for themselves." I had no idea what he meant.

Even so, that very day, that week, that month, that year, as I began to put these new ideas into practice, I could see the little miracles that Mike had told me would take place if I kept to my "I'm willing to do anything for peace" intention.

But, though everything I was learning felt right, every once in a while some part of me put up resistance.

You may ask why. Four reasons: I knew that everything I thought I knew would have to change. I knew that I'd have to take full responsibility for the mess I'd made of my life. I knew that, because of my unresolved emotional issues, my life was sure to get worse before it got any better. And here's the real kicker — I was frightened because I didn't want my new "I am God" attitude to piss God off. But I was determined to change, no matter what it took.

I began to meditate daily as Mike had said to do. I can honestly say that the more I practiced meditation, the more my life improved. That alone has helped me stop feeling like a victim and to live more in harmony with God.

Another thing Mike suggested I do was to train my senses to take in everything around me. To my astonishment, I noticed that whenever I consciously engaged one of my five senses, my sixth sense would make itself known to me. Before long, intuition became an everyday part of my life.

Let's just say that if it weren't for Mike's lessons and the support of my other dear Soul brothers, Chris and Jeff — well, I can't imagine what my life would be like now. I thank them daily in my prayers.

Nowadays, I think it is safe to say that I'm a changed man. I seem to be able to use what I've learned at any time to move me through whatever I'm facing. Occasionally I revert to my old ways and make things happen that I really wish I hadn't. Whenever such unconscious creations do show up, I'm lucky in the sense that I can always resort to all the knowledge I've gotten, beginning that night at Chris'.

One very important thing I've learned is how to take responsibility for whatever I do. And with that has come excitement, because now I finally get that I can have any- and everything I want if I keep on cleaning up my life. To stay on task, I daily ask God to open my heart and to keep reminding me that I can create Heaven within me any time I choose.

———◆———

Ever since I've realized that I am God, we are God, everything is God, I've experienced moments most people would call miraculous. And I've noticed that when I take the time to recognize God in others, my ego (that has always separated me from them) vanishes and better relationships are the result.

Maybe you're in the same place now that I found myself in years ago — confused, angry and without direction. If so, my first suggestion is to do as the title of this chapter says — look within. Take an inventory of how you feel about yourself and begin to see how the choices you have made have affected not only yourself, but others as well. When you begin to assume full responsibility for everything that happens to you, you will find yourself becoming imbued with the same kind of power I've found, and you will be able to consciously create your own life, as I am now able to do.

Here's something else for you to try. When you're around others, practice expanding your awareness outward. All you have to do is put your God-given senses to work and you'll begin to discover, as I did, the good in all things. Begin to feel. Begin to touch. Begin to see. Begin to listen. Begin to know. Begin to be. Begin!

Lastly, get back to basics. To help you do that, I now offer three tenets that have been (and are still) quite helpful to me, and that seem to be the foundation for my spirituality.

1) The all-knowing tenet: If turning inward unites me with God (Higher Self), then it makes sense to me that *Omniscience* (Peace) is my natural state.
2) The all-powerful tenet: If turning inward unites me with God, then it makes sense to me that *Omnipotence* (Love) is my natural state.
3) The all-pervading tenet: If turning inward unites me with God, then it makes sense to me that *Omnipresence* (Liberation) is my natural state.

The gift God has given to me I want to give to you. I take great pleasure in sharing with you my prophetic vision of Heaven on Earth.

You are the Vision, the Christ.
In truth, all there is *is* you.
Walk into your divinity.
Walk into the One.
You are
God
✡
† † †

May peace be with you.

Keith

*God-realization will happen
when you finally free yourself
from the brain, the senses,
the mind—the wanter.*

REALIZING GOD

This will be My final transmission in our book. But before I "go," I shall leave you with a guide for you to follow so that you will be able to reach your destination.

———— ◆ ·————

All who seek divinity must live a life free from wanting, for that is the source and cause of spiritual bondage. As long as one is constantly wanting, one will only fall farther away from the selflessness of Grace into the selfishness of ego.

The ego mind is the cloth that veils Consciousness — your wants are its threads. But when you give up your constant wanting, the ego-threads will fall away and the cloth will disappear, revealing your True Nature, the pure, genuine Self that is the Soul.

God-realization will happen when you finally free yourself from the brain, the senses, the mind—the wanter. Once you break out of your finite little prison of individuality, you will become conscious, enlightened—one with the Cosmic Power. Thus, will you reach God!

TWO FRIENDS
SHAKING HANDS

Well, that about wraps it up.
"Thanks for coming to me and sharing every-thing that You've shared."
You are most welcome. I ask you, Keith, why would I not?
"I didn't believe that such a thing could ever happen."
So I take it you realize that you still have work to do?
"Yes, and lots of it!"
A few years hence, if you are willing, what do you say we do this again?
"Absolutely! So who gets the last word?" (waiting)
... (still waiting)
... (finally realizing he's been had)

EPILOGUE

THE GIFT

Years ago, I got a gift
    from a wise and caring friend.
    Though I'd had it all along,
    I couldn't comprehend
    how big it was and yet so small;
    how it was there, yet not at all.

My friend said, "You're one of many
    who can change this special place."
    I could tell how much he meant it
    by the look upon his face.
    Then I went far away,
    where my Soul so longed to be,
    where no mind could imagine,
    no eyes could ever see.
    While I was there I wondered
    just how to use this thing.

Should I cause grownups to cry
or make the children sing?

I sat with my confusion
'til I knew just what to do —
as this gift was passed to me,
I pass it on to you.

But, though I give this gift to you,
It does not come from me.
The Gift is God Himself —
if you only choose to see!

PRAYER OF GRATITUDE

Heavenly Father/Mother God,
I am grateful
for all that You have bestowed upon me
in my life.
There is but one thing more I ask:
help me hold this gratitude and humility
within my heart,
now and forever.

Blessings for Food

Heavenly Father/Mother God,
I am grateful for this food.
I ask that You free it from all negativity
so that it may nourish my being,
so that I may do Your Will.

LOVE IS LIFE

Life is Love. Love is life.
Merge with God, transcend your strife.

Fear is false, though real it seems.
When you rise above it, you'll fulfill your dreams.

Yes, you have the magic, the power's your own,
when you know where you've been,
are now, and are going.

WHERE THERE IS...

Where there is Love, there is peace.
Where there is peace, clarity of mind.
Reach deep into yourself,
transcend your fear,
to touch the Great Divine.

Everywhere around you, Spirit shows Its face.
When you see life through the eyes of Love,
Truth unfolds through Grace.

A Lesson In Love

When I was child,
   I caught a young sparrow and held it in my hands.
It sang me a song of new birth —
   of innocence — of freedom and flight.
Though captured by the beauty of the moment,
   I was afraid to lose this tiny mirror of pure joy,
   so I put it in a cage to admire.

Days passed, but the sparrow rarely sang.
When it did, its song was no longer beautiful —
   it was a song of sorrow.

For the first time, I could see how my fear
   had imprisoned not only this little sparrow,
   but me as well.
It was then I knew I had to release it
   to fly away and be free.

I reached into the cage and gathered the sparrow
  into my hands more gently than before.
As I did so I said, "You have taught me
  how to sing my own song of new birth,
  of innocence, of freedom and flight.
Because of you, I've discovered the joy
  that was with me long before we met."

I thanked the sparrow for the love it had shown me
  with its simple act of allowance.
Then I raised the bird to Heaven and let it go—
  "Now fly, my little teacher, fly!"

ABOUT THE AUTHOR

Keith Blanchard was born on November 30, 1963, in Houma, Louisiana, and had a typical middle class Catholic upbringing. In his early teens, he often entertained himself by pondering the big questions about God and the universe. Little did he know that the day would come when those questions would form the spiritual foundation upon which he would build the rest of his life.

In his late twenties, Keith went through a crisis that stripped him of everything he held dear and left him with no choice but to turn inward for answers. This he did, but the peace and stability he so wanted still eluded him.

When he was thirty-two, celestial beings began to appear to him, sharing glimpses of his future and the world's. Not only did they enlighten and guide him, they instructed him to pass their message on to others so that they, too, could learn a higher way of living.

Now forty and living a peaceful, stable life, Keith continues to pursue his passion to both learn and teach about Truth.

Keith's credo:

Why choose to believe when you can know!

CPSIA information can be obtained at www.ICGtesting.com
Printed in the USA
LVOW110810021111

253074LV00001B/86/P